M
Archive

M
Archive

After the End of
the World

ALEXIS PAULINE GUMBS

Duke University Press   Durham and London   2018

© 2018 Duke University Press
All rights reserved
Printed in the United States of America on acid-free paper ∞
Designed by Heather Hensley
Typeset in Minion Pro by Tseng Information Systems, Inc.

Cataloging-in-Publication Data is available from
the Library of Congress.
ISBN 978-0-8223-7069-7 (hardcover : alk. paper)
ISBN 978-0-8223-7084-0 (pbk. : alk. paper)
ISBN 978-0-8223-7187-8 (ebook)

Cover art: Soraya Jean-Louis McElroy, *Ancestral Alchemy 1*, 2012–2013.

to the purveyors of our
bright black future

AFTER AND WITH

Pedagogies of Crossing
by M. Jacqui Alexander

CONTENTS

ix | A NOTE

3 | From the Lab Notebooks
of the Last Experiments

31 | Archive of Dirt: *What We Did*

71 | Archive of Sky: *What We Became*

89 | Archive of Fire: *Rate of Change*

105 | Archive of Ocean: *Origin*

133 | Baskets (Possible Futures
Yet to Be Woven)

185 | Memory Drive

213 | ACKNOWLEDGMENTS

217 | NOTES

227 | PERIODIC KITCHEN
TABLE OF ELEMENTS

A NOTE

She had to feel what it was like to survive above ground
while really living underground by fire. She had to come
as close to the ground as I did, learning to depend upon
the damp rain smell of earth to clean her insides, jar her
senses and to bring her to the heart of the oath I had sworn
never to betray: all life is shared with those at the bottom
of the Ocean. . . . This learning would take at least the span
of one life, and only the Soul could decide what would be
left over for a different time, a different place.

—Kitsimba describing Jacqui's work in
M. Jacqui Alexander's *Pedagogies of Crossing*

M. Jacqui Alexander's *Pedagogies of Crossing: Meditations on Femi-
nism, Sexual Politics, Memory, and the Sacred* (2005) is an ancestrally
cowritten text. This means that in addition to the interventions this
text makes in the ways we imagine transnational feminist account-
ability, movements from within the university industrial complex,
layers of time and space in quantitative research, postnationalist
Caribbean sexualities, radical feminist of color memory, and the
labor economics of spirit work, to name a few of the enduring inter-
ventions this text has made over the past decade, the book itself also
works to create textual possibilities for inquiry beyond individual
scholarly authority.

Kitsimba, a persistent ancestor who challenges Alexander's academic interpretations of her historical plantation resistance existence, chooses to school Alexander and to speak to her and through her, wryly resenting the employees who get credit for being Alexander's so-called research assistants. Unpaid in one sense, overpaid in others, I have also been a research assistant of M. Jacqui Alexander's. Along with Moya Bailey and Julia Roxanne Wallace, I had the honor of assisting Alexander while she was a visiting chair at Spelman College (at the same time that I was engaged in a dissertation research fellowship at Emory University). Alexander taught two courses—"Migrations of the Sacred" and "Black and Immigrant Women in the Land of Dollars"—crafted a digital migration story-sharing process between her Atlanta students and her Toronto students, and organized a two-day symposium called Africa in the Americas: Movement, Light, Sound and Water. Much of our time was spent troubleshooting technology, observing Alexander as she taught, and sitting on Alexander's living-room floor listening to the story of the migration of the *obi* oracle from West Africa through the New World. Soon after this time, Alexander left the academy to build a center for indigenous knowledge in Tobago.

In *Pedagogies of Crossing*, Alexander clarifies the middle passage of the transatlantic slave trade as an act of violence that continues to impact the entire planet through the indivisibility of the water, wind, earth, and fire that surround and constitute our world. She also suggests that the crossing was not only a geographic transfer of millions of people but also a movement of energies and elements into a relationship that persists, a material and conceptual relationship we navigate with the potential and compelled crossings we make in each moment. Periodically, then, in my text you will be confronted with the periodic table of elements, interacting with the organization of this text based on the impact, difference, and transformative potential of the material traces of this moment. At the end of the book a list of texts other than *Pedagogies of Crossing* that have had a chemical impact on this work are included for your continued engagement.

Honoring *Pedagogies of Crossing* as an ancestrally cowritten text and an ancestor to this book, *M Archive: After the End of the World* imagines another form, speculative documentary, which is not *not* ancestrally cowritten but is also written in collaboration with the survivors, the far-into-the-future witnesses to the realities we are making possible or impossible with our present apocalypse. This book centers Black life, Black feminist metaphysics, and the theoretical imperative of attending to Black bodies in a way that doesn't seek to prove that Black people are human but instead calls preexisting definitions of the human into question. It depicts a species at the edge of its integrity, on the verge or in the practice of transforming into something beyond the luxuries and limitations of what some call "the human." Will the future witnesses of this crossing know themselves as human? This book offers a possibility of being beyond the human and an invitation into the blackness of what we cannot know from here.

In other words, this speculative documentary work is written from and with the perspective of a researcher, a post-scientist sorting artifacts after the end of the world. This is you beyond you. After and with the consequences of fracking past peak oil. After and with the defunding of the humanities. After and with the removal of people of color from the cities they built. After and with Audre Lorde. After and with Toni Cade Bambara. After and with Barbara Christian. After and with Nellie McKay. After and with June Jordan. After and with Cheryll Y. Greene. After and with Gloria Naylor. After and with Jayne Cortez. After and with Lucille Clifton. After and with Kitchen Table: Women of Color Press. After and with the Combahee River Collective. After and with clean water. After and with handwriting. After and with a multitude of small and large present apocalypses. After the end of the world as we know it. After the ways we have been knowing the world.

M is for Mary and Maryam and Moses and make-believe. *M* is for McKenzie. *M* is for miracle and mayhem and mass incarceration. *M* is for migrant and microcosmic and major. *M* is for magic and metastasization. *M* is for muscle and memory and mitochondria. *M* is for minor and malevolence and manna. *M* is for maternal and mule and music. *M* is for meal and minute and mandrill. *M* is for mammal and makeup and mercury. *M* is for must be and maybe and much.

Consider this text an experiment, an index, an oracle, an archive. Let this text be as alive as you are alive. Might be enough.

it's hard to say what the people did. because as usual there was no "the people" there were only people. but all the people thought they were part of "a people" which was rightly "the people" even when they weren't sure anyone else had survived.

so different people did different things. but, for a time at least, they all thought they were the only people left alive, and so they documented what happened with them as if it were the whole record. that's the historiographical problem.

which is not to say the remaining survivors were ignorant or proud or separatist or that they *wanted* to be the only people. but a major part of their sense of the situation depended on their understanding that everyone else was dead. according to the radio waves that we can still find floating around here sometimes, some of them did reach out and state their locations to see if there was anyone else checking. but we don't actually have evidence of signal reading.

i like to think there were some readers though. descendants of those ancients who kept their computers on listening for responses from so-called extraterrestrials. there had to be some good listeners left alive.[1]

From the Lab Notebooks of the Last* Experiments

*Last is a verb

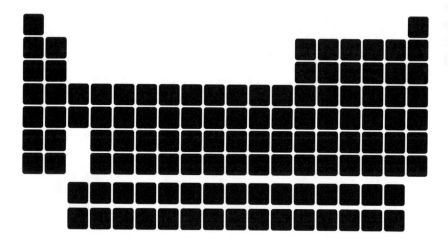

divide by the deaths you had to metabolize yesterday. divide by the shot echoes in your dreams. divide by the sleep you didn't get thinking you had to hustle harder. divide by the water you didn't drink either.

multiply by every pore touched, every memory made skin again, every word of love and the lips that share them. multiply by the sound of children. the sound that never stops. exponent of the will of the ancestors which will be dreamt. but not slept through.

all things are not equal.
wake up.[1]

this thing about one body. it was the black feminist metaphysicians who first said it wouldn't be enough. never had been enough. was not the actual scale of breathing. they were the controversial priestesses who came out and said it in a way that people could understand (which is the same as saying they were the ones who said it in a way that the foolish would ignore, and then complain about and then co-opt without ever mentioning the black feminist metaphysicians again, like with intersectionality, but that's another apocalypse).

the Lorde of their understanding had taught them. *this work began before I was born and it will continue . . .*

the university taught them through its selective genocide. one body. the unitary body. one body was not a sustainable unit for the project at hand. the project itself being black feminist metaphysics. which is to say, breathing.

hindsight is everything (and also one of the key reasons that the individual body is not a workable unit of impact), but if the biochemists had diverted their energy towards this type of theoretical antioxidant around the time of the explicit emergence of this idea (let's say the end of the second-to-last century), everything could have been different. if the environmentalists sampling the ozone had factored this in, the possibilities would have expanded exponentially.

that wouldn't have happened (and of course we see that it didn't) because of the primary incompatibility. the constitutive element of individualism being adverse, if not antithetical to the dark feminine, which is to say, everything.

to put it in tweetable terms, they believed they had to hate black women in order to be themselves.

even many of the black women believed it sometimes. (which is also to say that some of the people on the planet believed they themselves were actually other than black women. which was a false and

impossible belief about origin. they were all, in their origin, mainte-
nance, and measure of survival more parts black woman than any-
thing else.) it was like saying they were no parts water. (which they
must have believed as well. you can see what they did to the water.)

the problematic core construct was that in order to be sane, which is
to live in one body, which is to live one lifetime at one time, which is
to disconnect from the black simultaneity of the universe, you could
and must deny black femininity. and somehow breathe. the funda-
mental fallacy being (obvious now. obscured at the time.) that there
is no separation from the black simultaneity of the universe also
known as everything also known as the black feminist pragmatic
intergenerational sphere. everything is everything.

they thought escaping the dark feminine was the only way to earn
breathing room in this life. they were wrong.

you can have breathing and the reality of the radical black porous-
ness of love (aka black feminist metaphysics aka us all of us, *us*) or
you cannot. there is only both or neither. there is no either or. there
is no this or that. there is only all.

this was their downfall. they hated the black women who were them-
selves. a suicidal form of genocide. so that was it. they could only
make the planet unbreathable.[2]

and then there was the muscle called the heart. at one stage of human history they liked to say it was the size of the fist. this was one way they admitted how central extremity was. and the fist-lifting people were sincere. they imagined that they could show their hearts, lift them up and out of their chests, make their blood flow vulnerable and coordinated. that's what they meant.

but of course it was as anatomically irrelevant as those european medieval anatomists who insisted that the heart was directly in the middle of the body, or that the stomach was the organ of love, or even those patriots who imagined the heart always already on the right side of the chest.

what we have to remember about the human heart is that yes it was a muscle. yes it was central. yes it was vulnerable when it was. and so when the toxicity of the species developed to the point where extremities started freezing and falling off. (you'll remember that one of the first results of the fracked water was deep interruptions in circulation.) the idea of the heart had to change.

the engaged heart, temporarily measured by small machines that people wore to count their steps and movements and calories, developed a counter-rate that communicated something other than the conditioning of the individual. it ticked like the urgency of action. and so in the end, those specific people who had used the colloquial name for the heart "ticker" were closest to being right.

and of course at this point it goes without saying that they were (to be colloquial again) running out of time.[3]

they never proved it, but we know. some of the hand-waving women had always known. some of the metaphysicians had been trying to say. no one took them literally. until the earth broke apart.

and then. with the probe technology, with the accurate diagrams. with the skilled cave divers going deep into the fault lines. and with the simultaneous release of the human heart project and the lateral lobe mapping, it became impossible to ignore.

the cracks where the earthquakes expressed themselves were exactly the same contours of the fissures in our minds and the breaks. all the breaks. in our hearts.[4]

they had this thing about darkness. the bottom of the ocean, outer space. they were afraid of it, they wanted to penetrate it. they wanted to pretend it only existed in contrast to light. and there was something about not wanting to have their eyes closed. not wanting to go within. lightweight enlightenment equaled mass black death.

so through the accidents of scholarships, the trickle-down of diversity funding, and the calling from spirit that was before and behind and up under all of that, the black oceanists emerged. and the black oceanists trained themselves and each other not to be afraid of going black (that was what they called it) for days at a time. they were not afraid to slow and evolve their breathing. they were not afraid of their kinship with bottom crawlers who could or could not glow. they were not afraid of being touched by what they could never see, never bring back to the light, never have a witness for.

or to be more precise. they knew about that already. and they were less afraid of the underwater unknown than they were of the blatant dangers up on land.

so the second skin they put on to dive was thick and black, but not quite as thick, nowhere near as constricting as what they already knew.

they showed each other their teeth. drunk and daring on what the unknowable would teach them. and it was not long before they started to long for longer, to plan for a plan that would sustain generations below. depth of a plan that didn't require, include, value, or chart a return to the surface ever again.[5]

they were the first ones who learned to light themselves and find each other. the critical black marine biologists, scientists of the dark matter under fathoms, suggest that there may be a causal relationship between the bioluminescence in the ocean and the bones of the millions of transatlantic dead. oyeku ogbe. they have been studying the relationship between blackness and light. which is not to say that before the face of god or the race of capital moved across the deep there was no light within the deepest sea creature, but is instead a signal to remember the character of calcium. the meaning of the presence of magnesium. both of which catalyze bioluminescence.

don't let me lose you. they are not saying that the light in the deep or the stars at the bottom of the sea didn't exist before the weight of the bones of the captives who would not live as captives. before the introduction of the diving shark-cleaned bones of the free into the complex environment of the one inseparable ocean. they would never say that.

but who would suggest an origin for light, except blackness.

what the dark scientists are saying is that now that the bones are there as fine as sand, the marrow like coral to itself, the magnesium and calcium has infiltrated the systems of even the lowest filter feeders. so any light that you find in the ocean right now cannot be separated from the stolen light of those we long for every morning. and I don't need to remind you that the ocean, that place where the evolutionists and creationists all agree that life began, the source of all the salt we breathed to get here, lives within us.

all light is shared with those at the bottom of the ocean.[6]

remember the frogs.

after everything we had tried to say to prove that human was human beyond gender. after people had cobbled together the bodies of loved ones out of rubble that didn't segregate or care. after the water content and the advocacy advance led to historically unprecedented numbers of proud intersex leaders. after the pronoun transformation and the protests and the institution building and the ostensibly safer spaces, we let that go and took a different approach. we liked to think of it as an evolutionary approach. and really at that point what could anyone do with this rising water but emulate the amphibians. what we had done to the planet made us crave and need a bothness of slick skin and webbing and genital adaptability.

they say that it was deep in the ocean that certain fish learned to self-fertilize. or that after the ice age the remaining amphibians evolved how they needed to. and if any species knew how to decimate habitat, i mean how to zone ourselves out of safe space for contact, it was ours right? or what we had been. and our range of ancestors moved beyond the eunuchs to a more ancient and just as relevant set of references. some said it would be the extremely logical end point of our individualism and ownership: self-impregnation. but we, the evolutionaries, knew it was just as valuable as transparent water-proof skin over your eyeballs. we could become whoever we needed to be for each other.

we created the future in form.[7]

the only precedent was gallstones. or maybe (according to some critical black oceanographers) pearls. how the smallest piece of sand can transform you until you organize your life around the pain. hard shell almost impossible to pry open, but inside everything soft, naked, new. except the rock. the round and hard place they were built around.

turns out i shine my fear with all of me, keep it moist and fed and perfect. tend to it and tiptoe around like it's a newborn baby. it's not. it has been here much longer than i have. someone else has cared for it before. it seems like it gets more precious with the passing years, but that's wrong.

when they came to the planet looking for traces of the humans we had been, all they found were these round and gleaming stones. it was poetic for them, given the shape of the planet itself. given all the water so close to the expanding sun. if we could have seen it, maybe we would have found it more poetic than ironic too. the planet shone with all our perfectly round fears and how we left them.

i hope they build iridescent shrines. i hope they decorate a path to dreaming thrones. i hope they make a rainbow waterfall of marbles. or reflect passion into action with pinball confidence and speed. make something out of who i never was. have fun with it. the fear that made me whole.[8]

they began to study the death of the black artist. strung out the veins on tables to dissect them. looking for the impact of ink, early mornings, and that repeated refusal to be silent. they wanted to know if there was physiological weight to the common perception that their ancestor portals were enlarged, and if so, what swelling, what inflammation bore the evidence of that transit. did it crowd the other organs out for example? cause the liver to work harder or less?

what was in them that made work more food to them than food was? and tobacco? was it indigenous memory? how often did they paint their insides with substance and strain? is there an imprint that deepens in the face of repeated misunderstanding and tokenization? does it inoculate the blood?

what they found gave them pause. but they published a cursory article on "ego and the black artist" to comply with the funding. and most of them moved on to other things. and didn't tell each other that they never slept through the night again. it wasn't until your girl nanine (the great scientist) came back at and looked through the records that she shook her head and drew up the next phase.

"prototype for eternal life serum: phase indigo."[9]

and then there was the melanin. long after the artists learned to full body tattoo their skin every color of the rainbow, the melanin started to matter more. again. it was as if the sun had moved closer, but really we had simply burned up everything between us and that nearest star.

and when, at a major loss to vulnerable test subjects, they discovered that melanin itself could *not* retain its sun-protective powers once extracted, Africa began the last era of its resource-rich life. what was a rich dark continent without the utility of extraction? the world bank economists gave up on trying to predict what it meant.

and when light-skinned women started to have trouble finding darker-skinned partners, the seasoned advertisers in the magazines had to retire. what did paleness mean as a physical liability with no discourse strong enough to elevate it? even dominicans started putting dirt on their faces.

this is how the story we had used to justify the full-scale destruction of the world outgrew itself at last. but was it too late?[10]

the question for the neuronationalists was how to wash out the trauma without wiping away the skills we had built around all that hurt, all that longing, all that loss. and when they figured that out. well you had no chance. but we still had to live with the consequences.

so they went in like the eternal sunshine movie, like our brains were video-game landscapes, and they hunted. they could chart the steady erosions of certain regions of our minds where we thought of you and what you had done. well not directly. the easiest thing was to find the places where the skills we had built to survive what you had done made hatch marks on our lobes. ruts, you might say. the depth of our resistance, the evidence of your erstwhile irrevocable presence.

during the time when we win no matter what. this is your last survival. how winning how we win still hurts from you.[11]

it was no longer a matter of sex.

this new molecular relationship made *distance* and *intimacy* words
that tangled.
or to say it another way.
we were all close.
beyond close.

not knowing where one person ended and another began was no
longer love-song advertising or evidence of codependency.

it was a real issue. so then identity ($x = x$) was no longer technically
true. the previous energetic reality of how we are not whole and
change each other and are not ourselves except in the most lim-
ited version of our imagination became impossible to ignore on
the physical level.

so love was not about merging or finding exceptional moments
when we could die enough to shrug off the pain of individuality.
it was just a certain sound, a vibration, and when we achieved it,
it was really all of us.[12]

they blew up the sand to sort it. wearing lenses that magnified the world to 360 times its size, they found that sand was not sand anymore and the thing about the stars in the sky and the grains of sand was more poetic than the ancients could have known. (or did they know?) each piece of sand its own world of color, shape, size, symbol, and meaning. a purple starburst, a green coil, a golden cylinder. as if they had all been made for a different magic. and so they sorted them by type. they sifted through. the only use left for the most basic thing they had learned to do. those who wanted to continue to live that way, to use all the sorting and differentiation instinct they had built up over the years. that's all it was good for at that point. sorting sand.

what i would have told them, if i thought they could listen, was the same thing i told anyone who seemed to listen. that of course the sand was visibly different. sand is what sand is. tiny remnants of fossils and stones and planets and shells all broken beyond recognition. unless you look closer, unless you magnify each by 360 degrees, unless you become intimate and positively obsessed. and then you see where they come from, whole in their being. you see more possibilities than you thought you could see.

there is a lesson there about what we have broken down into and what has not broken us, how similar we look from a distance, how we stay being whatever we came from, what attention does and what it does not do, how we all become sand in the end.[13]

they went back to nature to describe it. ironically and too late. it was a beehive, a honeycomb, geometric and stuck together. it was life sutured by death enforced by drones.

or it was a coral reef. bright with tiny tentacles and built on the bones of the dead turned brittle with their living turning white and craving moss to mark memorial.

or it was spanish moss draped like shawls on live oaks, draped like death on display, hanging limp like its power could be pretended away.

they wanted to say that the relationship between the living and the dead was natural.
they wanted to find a way to say that.[14]

nobody signed anything. and the witnesses were accidental. nobody could think of recruiting someone to arbitrate. and plus. the usual arbitrators were gone. or leaving on whatever terms they could negotiate with wind and heat and thirst. later some will wonder why they didn't use the technologies they had developed to track the movement of birds, the migration of turtles, or the strategic gatherings of fish. but if you had been there you wouldn't ask that question. they already knew they were beyond understanding. nothing natural to see here at all.[15]

some people said it was the strings of the kora, how they trained
their hands to know the right moment. some people said it was no
harp it was heartbeats stopping. the ethnographers of the poetry of
math presented research that explained the correlations between
the intervals of death, the number of bullets discharged, the numer-
ology of the names of the jurors, the weather in the area on the day
of the shooting, the estimated number of total heartbeats of the
shot. you could only divide them by seven and three, which meant
you could not divide them without reaching a crossroads or an
ocean. so that was how they knew where to go.[16]

in the end it was triangulation. they specified how different they were from each other until they could extrapolate and find god.

in the end it was a false triangle. they tried to chart god and kept getting back to themselves. they tried to chart each other and kept getting back to themselves. they tried to chart themselves, but how could that be objective?

in the end it was the Pythagorean theorem inverted. not this squared plus that squared equals the long side of hell squared. aka the way squared subtracts where you thought you started squared from where you'll never go squared. turns out it's not a square at all. it's a circle. if you put a triangle in the middle the edges either won't touch or will exceed the given space.

actually, it was not a circle, it was a sphere. it was not just a sphere, it was a globe. it was not just a globe, it was a planet with its own destiny. wasn't it? and the triangle didn't fit and the pyramids were pointing somewhere with the queens and treasures dead inside.

from here? i don't know. from here? i just don't know.[17]

when she said the mud mothers she meant that energy close to the core of the earth where the planet felt more alive, soft, hot, and in production. if you could look close enough (or listen carefully enough, the critical geologists would have corrected), you could see the churning planet making herself brown. if you were to choreograph a dance about it (which, i agree, would be an excellent idea), you would need to have everyone cover themselves with mud and then make motions like pushing, like freeing wrists, but lead with the belly, their legs should be far enough apart to let them squat and rise back up, like if they were pushing time forward and feeling it push them back, and they would eventually get closer and closer together until you felt like you were watching one being, growing together curving home and pressing pressing to solid but still always breathing. (it will be good, when you recruit the dancers, if some of them are pregnant.)[18]

it was the salt. she wants us to know. it was the salt. final repository of the shore and salt of home. we were preserved and packaged flesh. we were reduced to our salt. chemical archeologists have run projections on the ships by now. accounting for the ocean. accounting for the wreck. accounting for the centuries of neglect. they estimate that the air in the hold was as many parts saline as oxygen. but you could have asked anyone sitting on the porch back in her day. there were spaces we made in our palate to preserve what preserved us. be it blood, water, waste. be it sweat, tears, or secretions. be it breathing or decomposition. what she knew was that if the body could gather enough salt, it could stay. it could stand anything. it could reconstitute the stolen soil in vein. *taste* is not a big enough word to hold it. what we went through.[19]

it got to the point where she could close her eyes and map the universe. stars dying, voids reversing, oceans freezing on planets far away. she could find it all somewhere inside.

sounds beautiful, but it was inconvenient. why should she wake up in the middle of the night just because a volcano erupted on a planet orbiting another star? why should she cry in the middle of a conversation just because the poles of some poor planet were melting into oceans?

she began to hate the word *middle*.

and the fake scientists who, of course, had never understood dark matter had colonized space in their imaginations. and it was all too easy for them to confine her to infinite tests. to place electric nodes on her smallest muscles. to link her breathing to twelve different computer monitors in twelve different offices. sometimes despite all the noise she would fall asleep and know that saartje was holding her hand.

meanwhile the real scientists, marooned to their asylums, overpasses, and parks, knew something was off. the trackers were not quite quantum in their calculations, not quite witnessing because of the way they had been trained. the real scientists spoke about it and nobody listened, but they kept talking, knowing the recording would rewind eventually.

the universe always knows when she is being disrespected. she is patient, but she is not *the* patient. and so lightning struck where it had to, and all the monitors linked to dark flesh went dark. and homegirl just quietly walked away. content never to be in the middle of anything. committed to always be in the middle of everything.[20]

they found them. the dream rooms and the body doubles and it made sense. rooms filled with sounds of water, crackling heat rooms, rooms with dirt walls and wide rooms like the widest air shaft you ever saw. they had thought themselves the owners of their bodies. their minds sovereign in a specific space and time. there was a break in the line when they discovered they were less and more at once.

imagine touching your hand to your hand and knowing that you and the whole world that you can perceive are the projection of a dream machine made out of the sleeping minds of people whose bodies look just like yours. *what happens when they wake up?* you have to think. *what and when am I really?* you must wonder. *how did their dreams make rooms to dream in? whence their peaceful bodies, whence their instantly activating minds?*

but more than that, the investigative scientist asked the self that might have been listening, looking at the slightly moving eyelashes of her beautiful double. *i mean what if she changes her dream?*[21]

when we started to find the imprints it was almost time. scattered around the planet (like we were) the shapes of our exact elbows our pressed cheekbones indented like fossils showed up on the ground and in the walls of caves as if by the chance (and the very unlikely chance at that) that we would find them.

were they left as messages? who left them? us? time started to match itself up, not so long after we started wandering everywhere to dig. when had we, the selves who became archeologists, decided to prove to ourselves that we had been time travelers first. and what would we do with the signs that were ourselves?[22]

it started as an old april fools' joke that none of us are old enough to have witnessed.

there was a kingdom called google. kingdom google bought the planet by managing the information and helping no one have to remember anything anymore. and the empire, called google, managed most of the information that people sent digitally to each other through machines. (are you following me?)

yes. it was like telepathy. but at that point they needed these machines to access their own telepathy. that's what a sad state, meaning planetary moment, it was.

anyway, the vast majority of the communication was digital before it became telepathic. the major change our ancestors experienced was the change from paper to digital, which was as unimaginable and overwhelming to them in their time as the move to psycho-spiritual interpersonal storage is to us at this time. but nonetheless it was totally dominant. almost every human on the planet had or wanted access to a digital device. it was how they externalized their thinking.

so what was the joke? i am getting to it. one day on april fools' (it's a fertility day they celebrated because they knew without saying it that laughter and humiliation led to more heterosexual shame sex). one day on april fools', the empire called google decided to pretend that they were starting a new service called "paper" where they would materialize the digital communications flying through their zone of influence (which was planetary and total as far as they knew) and send them through the "postal service" (the previous rulers of the empire of information).

it functioned very well as a joke, and it both reminded the subjects how much they loved the speed and lightness of digital communication and provided a kick in the teeth to the actual postal service, which for some reason still existed but was at that time going bankrupt.

you don't know the historical context so the joke isn't funny, but the joke is not the point. i am telling you the story of the baskets, not the story of the joke. the joke was just the accidental spark. late capitalism, the whole thing was a bad, clever joke with a cruel duration. and we have reclaimed our laughter for better more beautiful purposes by now. i hope.

i need you to know that the empire called google and its other digital allies would never have actually done this "paper" thing they were joking about doing. it was a joke. not a threat. though the joke of capitalism threatened everything that it did not outright destroy.

the digital empire depended on the interconnective intuition we already had, but the development of intuition was also a threat. what could make digital products obsolete faster than a telepathic market? in fact they were engaging all of their workers in the practice of imagining more and more ways to make their own digital services less and less intuitive. by training the people out of intuition and into internalized dependence on digitally externalized invisible connection, they sought to make their influence indispensable and eternal. we know how that went.

but anyway. one of our ancestors, who it turns out was also a descendant of the legendary stagecoach mary, was inspired by the joke. she saw it as a threat, in a way that was exactly opposite of the intention of the joke and the general response to it (most people laughed and forgot about it by april second).

this person (let's call her "mary") felt called and compelled to make the joke real. it was the only way to unyoke the joke. *what if,* she said, *every digital communication flying through wireless wires were to have a material counterpart receivable through the obsolete mail service or hand to hand through the redistribution of found objects.* mary especially loved to use popsicle sticks (maybe because of their saliva residual). and yes she really talked like that. on pieces of used paper, discarded clothes, trash of all kinds, mary started making a tangible and dirty archive of the clean digital world.

well, google had zillions and mary was only mary so she had to get help. she had to induct people into her practice, but it was actually not that hard. there were many people who craved a return to paper but who had been ashamed to admit it in front of the few remaining trees. mary's reminder that the most abundant resource of the google generation was still trash (often in the form of boxes shipped by the almighty ally amazon) changed everything. and they got on board and they brought down the messages from the cloud into the crowd in rather disruptive and beautiful ways, i must say. some of the most talented hackers joined mary and so even government secrets and encrypted lab experiments were floating around on sweetly placed candy wrappers and the like. and so that is how the tradition was born that ultimately led to this thing we are doing now.

this is how the story of the apocalypse ultimately got in our hands.

okay. that's lesson one.[23]

Archive of Dirt
What We Did

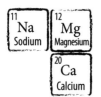

they came with sugar not of sugarcane
sweetness not of cotton but of air
they came with cakes not funneled down to grease
with layers like clouds
they came every day like it was their birthday
or yours
one or both
that was when they first came

and then they came with salt
with water and blood to wash you
they came with spit and sand to shine you
they came with cleansing first in mind
and woke your soul with it

next time they come
i hope they bring soil and green
soothe for the roots
i hope they bring dirt and depth
and plant us in it
we could sure use the grounding
for remembering earth[1]

from the surface archive

not big and blue. they were small brown women. the way their hair was silver heaven the way their skin was deep brown earth and how its texture mapped hills and valleys and tributaries of grace. it was there for anyone to see, really. or anyone to hear in the heightening or deepening tones of their voices, in the shaking vibration of their wisdom. if the people could not listen to the air all around them, if they could not place their hands on the cracked earth and know, they would only have had to pay attention to the small brown women who demonstrated it every day in language and action. not through perfection and wisdom. just through transparency. the beautiful and fragile ones who had no energy for hiding. how they moved slowly through the necessary with patterned regularity.

anything they wanted to know about the earth and what would happen if they ignored it, they could have learned by watching the old, curved brown women everywhere. but mostly they ignored those women. just like they ignored the world shaking around them. to their doom.[2]

they began to pity the rooted ones, because they did not understand.

meanwhile, on every level. the rooted ones grew. some called them tree people for the way they stayed planted, grew horizontally, shed colorful revelations every season onto the same ground. every winter they would bare their souls unafraid.

and their roots grew deeper and their branches reached out.

and the people who pitied them had no idea that their intimacy with the particular soil of their commitment allowed them to communicate underground, that the pressure of their pacing in the same spaces over again had a resounding impact that gained nuance until they could stay right where they were, take two steps back and forth in front of their homegrown altars, and depending on the direction and the rhythm of the steps, the speed of the turn, the weight, the rooted people elsewhere could know the message. how could the laughing people on the move know how the rooted people were making the internet obsolete?

and their roots grew deeper and their branches reached for sky.

you have to understand that this is after no one wanted the land. when the erstwhile speculators had ceased believing there would be a profitable future. when the would-have-been slumlords were busy with their spaceships or panic rooms and the dispossessed white children had turned to laughing to keep from crying and really had no energy left with which to gentrify effectively. staying power gained a whole new meaning when they saw there was no time for a white longevity mortgage.

by the end, the ones who stayed were the ones who could not leave. they stayed. with all their genius. and their archives of funeral programs.

their roots grew even deeper and their knowing branched up.

the rooted people latched their chakras to stars and stood in the light at angles and offered light projections on dark places in the

universe that telescopes had never paused upon. their names rang
from asteroids. their breathing grew the abyss.

the depth of root. the capacity to grow.

the mobile people shook their heads as they left and left and left.
they didn't know.[3]

a blogger compared them to the buckingham palace guards. but that wasn't quite it.

they stood. and they were silent. that much is true. and they were not fazed by the taunts of the people who were drawn to them by fear of their own stillness. but they were definitely not protecting the idea of a queen. or maybe they were. depending on what queen means to you.

and they were present.

that was what caused the taunters to shudder and the eventual pilgrimages of the more thoughtful folk. who all started to feel their questions were answered even though no one had moved a muscle.

it was said when you looked into their eyes you could feel them looking right into you. and silences inbetween your organs and in the darkest corners of your heart started to move, like everything was up for circulation again.

theories started to show up. that the land they stood on had been a burial ground. that they all had prosthetic legs. that there were people on hand with their hands to massage their calves at secret moments, but they were never called on. that they were actually blind and had been trained underground. or in a classified tank at the bottom of the ocean.

it was very hard to make generalizations about their skin, their hair, their piercings and markings. no one ever mentioned a gender or size. but then again it was also hard to look anywhere but their eyes. and you couldn't tell them apart because they carried the same energy. people never reported an encounter with "one of them" they only spoke of "they" and of "them," the pronouns were sufficiently neutral and plural and they were the only ones anyone used when they wrote about it.

there were contradicting reports that the people were naked, or they were clothed, or they were facing outward in a circle or they were facing east in a line, or they were facing whichever direction the sun or the moon was in. when the reporters were pressed to be specific they had to admit, they really didn't remember.

they stood. and they were silent. that's what we know.[4]

and then came the time of the water bearers, who had tuned their lower backs to the tone of distance. women who had been carrying water miles through cracked heat were the experts, their daughters born with the tendency for muscle strength in their calves, their upper arms, their heads shaped early for the indentation of the heavy empty sky.

the next generation developed a carrying style at womb level, cradling water as if water was just what it was. looking at the reflections of their own faces for balance. it became a ritual of thirst. and where the people had looked to create children in their own image, they began to notice their images already owned and lent back to them by water. water governed everything. and what we had done to water made the question of children secondary at best.

there was one dj named narcissus who tried to replicate the tired rhythms of their feet across the dust, tried to trace a treble line as transparent as water and to measure whether the movement of hips and the tides of the ocean had a ratio in common. she released the mixtape for free under the title, *will the children of the west ever pay their water debt?*

and at the remaining sites they listened and debated it. how could they ever repay the impact they had on water, the way divestment had turned the rivers into cesspools, the way corporations had eradicated the functionality of public water systems. Coca-Cola alone would have to invent a free purification system, build spaceships fast enough to go to the next solar system and import stolen water from elsewhere in the galaxy to even touch a tenth of what they had done.

it was ultimately the water that transformed how they thought of the concept of debt. it was the face of death reflected on the water that taught the spoilers and wasters what the women who had been carrying water through the twentieth century knew all along.

the distance is the distance. the body is the body. the water will not wait. there is no debt that can be repaid.

and they looked at their own faces, brown as the years went. and trusted in the shape of their eyes. and their dry drunk dredged-up dreams.[5]

after tigris and euphrates got names it became crass and territorial. men (like what men would one day turn dogs into) irrigating the periphery with sewage. that was not the point at all. and though the species, in its rush to dominate other species and its specified self, forgot the meaning of water, water never forgot itself. and indeed the controlling interest of water within the bodies of the people caused an unceasing longing that all the retraining and rebranding in the world could not completely kill.

millennia later, the maimed reality was that enough of the people thought they were 60 percent cola and enough of the people were cut off from their closest water supplies by the pollution and extraction of the companies owned by the cola producers that the longing turned autoimmune. it hurt too much to feel. the quite basic and natural longing for water became a symptom. pathologized and as expensive as the combined expenditure of every hospital in the world multiplied by the excess areas where the untreated and ignored shat the shit of the dehydrated directly into the remaining water supply. with an exponent of five. that number, it turns out, has a repeating decimal of seven. that's how we round up here.

and despite everything, because of everything, when it all went down they remembered to move towards water. or they moved towards water in order to remember. the order itself is unclear. but they headed down towards the groundwater and to the nearest coasts and to hidden and remembered rivers and to the places the rivers would have been if they had not been dammed, which is not that different from how it started, and the water said in the language of our longing bodies, *I knew you'd be back*.[6]

then they learned about dry. and how it really was water that kept the ground together, that kept their bodies together, that kept their teeth in their heads, when it stopped. they learned about salt and the brittle continents it made in the absence of what could be called rain. they learned about the elements and how they loved each other and how they raged to be apart. how a planet like any mother would cry until it couldn't cry anymore. they learned what dead skin cells felt like when there were no new cells to replace them. the mostly water people, ungrateful for their births, had found themselves, finally, in their own dust.[7]

she walked and she walked and she thought she would be able to put it down but she couldn't. thought the burden would get lighter, but it grew. how do you get the illusion of being light and carefree without actually giving up any of your hard-accumulated stuff?

you get a storage unit.

and this is what they did. until the planet was the perfect reflection of their crowded hearts. they felt unlovable. and the loads they carried always grew fatter than their muscles could keep up. this was not strength training, it was reverse conditioning. the acceptance of unacccptable conditions.

they got so good at it. first you had to drive all the stuff over to the place. a room locked next to many other rooms. then you could just fill up a pod they delivered to your very own doorstep, and not worry where they took it. just keep the prison number so they can bring it back when you want. one architect had an idea for chutes next to the trash room in big apartment buildings where you could label things to be taken to the region of your life you never visited and paid other people to defend. she disappeared before the application was complete, but by the end the gap was so big, there were sick and hungry children who would carry your necessary excess away for a very low fee. and they did a good job so you would use them again. of course sick poor children don't last long, so they had to be frequently replaced. but by the end, there were more sick children than places to put stuff.

in the end our burdens outgrew our strength.[8]

their small bones could have regrown from this, marrow being eager like it is. god paying attention like she should have been. we make our children into starfish. trust that they will reproduce their amputated smiles no matter what we show them. no matter what we show ourselves by risking them like this.

their small bones ultimately indistinguishable from plaster. we traded their lives to build these buildings. heated and cooled them as if they wouldn't need to breathe air. plumbed and drained them as if they wouldn't need water. we built these cities with the advance of their bones. which we knew would crumble under the weight of this. this is what we do. this is what we daily do. we violate the trust of being born.[9]

soon everything that was left had a half-life like hysteria. which meant our bodies were like landfills, places where nothing disintegrated but us. nothing made less of itself but the breathable air. and even the food should have been sad about it. becoming part of our bodies was not a transformative process. it was a holding pattern without a particularly scenic view.

and so the blockages and the growths and the ways our bodies turned against themselves were not curses or plagues from a disapproving daddy god, like some of the fundamentalists continued to say. the conditions of our bodies were simply reflections of the conditions of our storage units. and the conditions of our rain forests. and so the landfill actually became an ontology. the ontology.

simply put. every piece of the planet was filled with trash. our minds notwithstanding. our bodies included.[10]

it started on our tongues. everyone thought it was the water. the lack of water. the genetically processed seeds that didn't need water to thrive. or it could have been the post-ozone air. the tongue is sensitive like that. and we were living in a world that didn't taste right. that was for sure. so we explained the sores and tried to cure them with oil pulling and tonics.

it didn't work.

and once the sores got everywhere, on the bottoms of our feet on the palms of our hands, someone said it might have been our bloodstreams. bad blood with the planet recirculating through our straining hearts. some people even started to breed leeches.

it only got worse.

it hurt to move. it hurt to breathe. the food decline plateaued because it hurt so much to eat. and we were thick in our clothes from swelling. and when our eyes swole shut we couldn't see. and then we finally saw. we saw it.

we hadn't told the truth in so damn long.[11]

they were addicted to things like hydrogenated soybean oil and mutant chicken. their memories were linked to the tastes of things the studies said were poison. and so they bought other things, things that felt older to them. but they continued to trust the source of the studies, which was also the source of the earlier poisons. we can only understand this through the concept of addiction, which was an ancient condition of being that was characterized by lying to oneself and others in order to continue behavior that was repeatedly harmful to oneself and others.

they really thought they knew what home tasted like. what healthy was. how to cleanse their palates. there were brilliantly marketed packages that disavowed the past which were very attractive to people trying to distance themselves from the mistakes of their parents but who didn't have the bravery to distance themselves from the system that created their parents. they ate these new and different things while they pretended not to be their parents.

they thought they were tasting the future (which for some people tasted like cardboard and for other people tasted like sugar), but they were not. they were avoiding the necessary bitter tastes of the most accessible greens. to say the general palate was unbalanced would not be quite saying it. how could they have known what this would mean after?

the only ones who made it had a direct connection to those women who craved the crunch of eating dirt. who sensed their need for iron. and acted.[12]

they dug in their memories for the one day. for some of them it was a couple of days per month. rock-bottom days. the days in their lives when the world had already ended. they thought back. and asked:

what did we each do then? on the day that everything went wrong. when transportation and communication technologies conspired against us individually. when we personally couldn't get out of bed, dehydrated with crying. when we didn't ask for help. when we hurt the people we loved. when the sun died. when we lost everything. when we lost exactly who we needed to save. when we knew there would be no tomorrow. what did we each do then? how did we keep breathing past it (because we are the ones that did). they dug for those memories and stacked them in a row.

that's how. that's how we learned to get through this.[13]

each of us had to look it in the eye. the playstation, the hydroge-
nated soybean oil, before it was added to the pile of never again.
everything that required the small fingers of children for its manu-
facture. everything plastic releasing toxins all its half-life. the blood-
letting of our consumption was total.

and/or

one morning she looked in the mirror and saw all she had to give,
was all she had to give up,

that flesh she thought was hers.[14]

they attended to their fingertips. ridges and pulse. they channeled all their memory into their hands as if they knew what would happen to their brains and were determined to be able to make the world they needed from muscle memory. they believed in their reaching hands at least, that when the day came when they could not recognize themselves, at least some of their tired legs would lead them home and their open hands (their pulsing fingers) would be welcomed back again.[15]

then they learned to work with the soil they had. the daily dirt under their fingernails, the collected decomposition of their skin. they would have to grow what they needed from that. sometimes they remembered how many times caterpillars grow whole encasements of skin and shed them again and again before growing the skin that would become chrysalis. but nowadays they were focusing on a much smaller scale of organism. the bacteria swimming across the parched oceans of their eyes. the tiny cities in their intestine. the whole surface of their skins populated and evolving. this was the last step.

they finally had to understand themselves
as planets.[16]

and then there were the dirt-colored hands that had never held
money. field hands. marked hands of exchange. and grow and wait
and scrub and sometimes room and board or hot strained liquor.
those hands that wanted to do and make scratched with histories
of refusal.

there was worldwide confusion as to who exactly had been cursed
when their ancestors had made the sacrifice in blood and fire never
more to be slaves. and the brown eyes that had never held paper
or coins with watermarks of chains. the deep brown eyes that had
never shallowed to currency. the nuanced artists without the lux-
ury or the lash of abstraction. the washing well women who refined
reuse into ritual. at the end they already knew how to be brown and
thirsty and ha ha. free.[17]

they started with 33 for the number of bones in the spine. for the number of years of the sacrifice. for the symmetry. for the good luck resonance. who knows?

they started with 33 and each person became root calcium. bone protecting the last nerve of the planet that was through with us. attuned to every quiver.

they started with 33 and went into caves and found their own devils and faced them down.

they started with 33 and rotated pairs, mirroring each other. 16 and an external witness every time.

you can tell it how you need to tell it. the point is they started with 33. and it worked.

or

she sat on the floor with her curved spine tending towards the left and focused. she closed her eyes and told herself she could breathe into every bone and there would be space for the message.

there was.[18]

they crossed their hands in front of them, held each to the other and pulled back, exposing and lengthening muscles, tugging at the tension they needed in order to be able to grow.

no rings. every finger was for learning touch, learning how to be a hand, for palm reading each other's faces for selves, pasts, futures, and fuck-ups. and their feet were planted, each toe conscripted, pushing down as their heads reached diagonally up.

there were places the sun kissed them that they didn't know about. angles and star patterns ancients had built of stone. their bodies were repeating, not like reproduction, like the rhythm of a poem.

they could feel they were growing. biceps singing pulling in triceps teasing pulling out abs engaged. engaged the whole time.

if someone had told them that people used to buy each other down, strip each other into skeletons for the purpose of contracts and fear, they would have laughed.

and they were strong enough to laugh loud and for a very long time. without dropping each other on the ground.

and the ground shook, like the soil was trying to till itself when they looked into each other's open eyes.[19]

found underground

they started digging at the crossroads. some had called it the inter-section (mmhmm). and when they got through the pipes and the under-asphalt wire currents and the knotted tree roots and the gravel and grit and the cow footprints or whatever had been there before the blackening of pavement, they started to see the layers, the shells, the bones. they started to remember, they started to know, as they dug and they dug they got closer to home.[20]

when they dug they found figures they recognized, or wanted to recognize. they found the shapes of figures that they wanted to recognize *them*. this was back when they still wanted recognition. they made meaning out of the shapes of wooden boxes, the patterns of nails, the bones inside. they wanted to touch them and bag them and classify them. they wanted to analyze them for a connection to something older than death. but at the same time, they wanted to leave them to their rest and protest the fact that they had been disturbed yet again. this was before they really knew anything about rest, before they had a chance to experience it for themselves.

at that time they genuinely wondered (and it kept them up at night) whether rest was possible at all ever. even in death. even in death. uneven in death. black people were not safe.[21]

they started putting *x*'s on the places without treasure. without pleasure in their memories, without hope. sometimes all they had to mark them with was their own blood. sometimes the markings were as temporary as chalk, as sincere as cornmeal. this is how the ground looked as the people gave up. almost every spot a crossroads saying leave, this is no staying place. no place to dig for life or plant a question.

sometimes in their tired wandering the people would come across warnings in their own hands and they would shake their heads, feel stinging in their dried-out eyes, because here they were, back in a place they had marked unworthy of return.

that was when the people realized there had to be something after giving up, because there were no more places to leave. what do you do with a planet of excuses, scarred in unwelcome, inviting only absence? *X* marks the spot: not here.[22]

long ago they stopped asking the teenagers where they went at night. why they slept all day. where they put all that food. but they knew they were not dormant, they knew something was going on. in the meantime, those kids were working harder than anyone could have imagined. building livable environments in caves and aquifers. building the contingency world that no one knew we needed.

we marveled at it. we marvel at it still. who knew. literally no one knew. what all that sleepwalking could do.[23]

it became an abstraction *to stand up straight*. an infinitive that had
expired. certainly they could draw a human anatomy extended,
but the reality of underground living tilted them forward and they
could see their path. they could see their feet. they could see their
belly button with the slightest effort. it hurt at first, but then it didn't
anymore. and everything became much less linear. and instead of
the sun the core of the earth became the most studied and attractive
resource. they wouldn't have called it enlightenment. let's call it,
return.[24]

the glow got so great they could only sneak up after dark. and even then it might cause a total disruption. day instigation. the calling out of the remaining rooster descendants. the beginning of the surface work cycle off cue. the risk was a high noon from the depths of each. they had to hope that if they emerged and were spotted they would be dismissed as a flashback to ufo abduction syndrome by the rural transcendents. which is to say, the bold banked on their impossibility in order to move unseen bright as they were. it was not recommended. to emerge.

but that's not what matters. that's really not what matters. what i am trying to get at is that's how bright the inner light can get when it needs to in a situation of necessary darkness and total immersion in the material, which is to say, underground or at the bottom of the sea. and we cultivated it over generations. you need to understand that if you are going to put these in order. there was a time when "inner light" was a metaphor for something else. that might have been us, but this was not then.[25]

truth be told, she couldn't wait to get out from the surface, down past the sulfuric decimated air. the layer that protected the surface had been poisoned, now the only refuge was dirt. but not everyone could accept that. she learned slowly that the surface dwellers thought of themselves as clean. narrated their limited breathing capacity as refinements, whenever they had enough energy to talk. she always imagined brittle landscapes in their lungs, yellow as the ground they crawled, and sharp. monuments to desperation that stacked and broke off with their breathing. how else could you explain the rattling sound?

her elders were specific, only a certain number of hours aboveground. only a certain set of rehearsed answers about where she was from, who she was. and she should only use her full strength in an emergency. even this, they reminded her urgently (as if she could ever forget) was a major but necessary risk.

in another version of the story, she would have snuck extra time aboveground. she would have grown addicted to the open space and range of motion. she would have believed the lies the surface people told themselves and emulated them. or she would have pitied them so much she'd have to try to save them from themselves. maybe she would fall in love with someone her own age and realize that they weren't so different after all and environment wasn't everything. or do like the colonizers did and let pheromones override the visual, enough.

none of those things happened. she counted her seconds, like she was taught. she debated whether to tell anyone back below that aboveground was worse than they had described, worse than anyone had imagined. but she didn't want to seem like she was begging off the mission. it was only temporary, the elders promised. only a few more times. every time, she couldn't wait to get back underground.[26]

everything told them it wasn't time. the tint of the soil. the nakedness of the sky. what had they done with the clouds? what had they done to their own breathing? what had they done to the ground? what could ever support them now?

the scouts from the ones waiting underground retreated back through the caves. the brave ones who had been sent to check were cleansed with mud and sweet touches when they returned. they closed their eyes and sang until their skin stopped hurting. until their lungs felt clean again. they let their voices echo off the walls. this was their destiny. to wait and check. to let go of all of the what what what and to ask with their waiting. when?

when would the earthwalkers be ready for depth?[27]

from her memory

she felt it. just walking by. so she stopped and pressed her hand to the earth. this particular piece of earth was singing her name. she looked ahead to the miles of ruin and touched the memory of what she had seen on her way here and started to wonder. what was here. who was calling.

she sat.

she remembered the digging that had unearthed the African burial ground. she remembered the smooth floors of churches thick with prayer and the even smoother floors of slave dungeons thick with waste. she had long ago learned how spirit remains.

she didn't spend much time questioning how this particular piece of earth had become a magnet for her, because she knew the how of it from years of sensitivity. what she needed now during this empty day flanked by empty nights and dreams of the time before was to know the what of it. the whom.

so she sat. a long time. slowed her breathing and closed her eyes. and the memory built itself around her.[28]

she went to the studio of the murdered artist. built on the land of the decimated desert walkers. over the bones of the sky reptiles who had fallen that other time. *a fall is a fall*. she said, towards the end of summer, when the kids started to go back to school, but it was still a hundred degrees. and she found an indentation into earth shaped like earth itself when earth was a womb and she lay down in it, thinking tomb already dug. thinking just as well here as anywhere. and what she really wanted in that moment was to hear the ocean. and as she listened to her slow heartbeat and the full and wounded earth, seeking her own stillness, she learned instead that it was all still. it was all still there.[29]

this time she put her face directly in the dirt. no glasses to remove. no precious hair to pull back. no back to brace her to look up at the sky. just dirt. hard enough and soft enough to hold her. part of the day she pounded the earth with her fists and screamed blame and despair. part of the day she let soil slip through her fingers and felt comforted. most of the day she just acclimated herself to solid breathing and seeing all there was. which was brown.[30]

she pushed her fingers into the dust, wondering if anything could grow. if she had tears to cry maybe sea grape? if she had blood to spill maybe olive trees? if she could urinate maybe roses or something else with thorns? what is the plant strong and wrong enough for this situation? and what does it taste like, smell like when it grows?

her mother had remembered the names of the plants by what they did, bootblack, fever, toothache, the cures for problems they had faced in colonialism grew wild and pointless to anyone but the displaced. what could bloom here and what would they call it. is there a plant that can hold the total loss. scream tree, wailing grass, moaning root. she had to ask herself this question to deny the reason for it. what does a healer do after the last plant has abandoned? she pushed her fingers into the dust for now.[31]

they say she carried a root in her pocket. a root in her pocket every day.

they say the root was the only explanation for how she learned to walk that way.

they say she walked with a stiffness in her hips that taught them that she didn't play.

they say all those things about her because she didn't stay.

i wish i knew how to ask her
i wish she was here today.[32]

Archive of Sky

What We Became

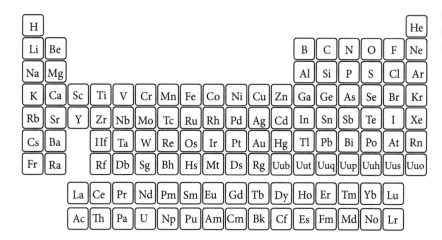

it wasn't like they lined up in rows and found each other at dawn. it was too late for all that. the front was scattered. almost metaphorical. which is to say the front was at the back of its implications. so that was the target. it would have been easier to hear the preparations than to see them. or better to read, if you could read. meaning if you could read the coded language of the air. the energy was shifting.

what meaning meant was meaningless. there were so many languages inside each language, such different meanings for each word, that the dialogical break was inevitable.

she had predicted this. even intended this. so she taught us to prepare for the incomprehensible in the best way she knew how. the poems.[1]

everyone knows we are made of stardust. they just don't remember what it means.

what does it mean?

it means if we can walk all over each other, we can also walk the sky.

like this?

like this.

*a conversation a couple of our ancestors had on a romantic night some time (but not too long) before they became constellations.[2]

remember when they did all those movies about zombies, but they
didn't include an afro-caribbean cosmology of death and servitude
and the people watched it nightly alone or together with their slick
popcorn or pretending to be together through interconnected video
games with surround-sound machine-gun noises?

when it happened it was not like that at all. and not only because
there was still no white savior.

after it happened it was hard to remember how we had walked
on this land and breathed this air before without the thickness of
knowing. they had always been here. every indigenous community
massacred, every single prophet assassinated, every child sacrificed
to colonialism, every slave rebel shackled in their grave, every un-
assigned body piled as refuse somewhere, had never disappeared.
whatever part they burned into air, whatever part they buried
underground, whatever part they threw in the sea, came whole again
in every breathing growing thing. and when the warning time came
they were all of them (all of them) screaming.[3]

at some point the work of pretending we weren't going to die, that our children weren't going to die, that our deaths and lives weren't going to be forgotten, became unsustainable. it was hard enough to just breathe and metabolize. to find something to metabolize. to find people to metabolize near. now some people call it the true end of whiteness, when the world could finally operate based on something other than fear of blackness, of being, of death. but at the time all we knew was the story had run out. all the stories. of staying young to cheat death. of thinking young people wouldn't die. of immortality via "making a difference." of genetic imprint as stability. of stacking money and etching names on buildings. people used to do those things before. not to mention that they would not mention death and would hide the dying away and strive to protect the eyes of the children who already knew everything.

at some point. all the dead being here anyway and all of us here being obviously doomed, we let go of that particular game. and started breathing. and saw our hands.

we let go.

i felt like i could fly.[4]

on a screen the size of a wall there was a gif of amazon warriors cutting off each other's breasts to better hold the weapons they needed.

through the speakers audre lorde's voice was on loop. the only recorded reading from *The Cancer Journals*.

she looked at her reflection, lit by candle in the small pool, and thought back to yesterday when her sister comrades had surrounded her singing, *I'm gonna lay down my burdens . . .*

she blew out the candle and began to pray. *may that which is not mine fall away. may that which hinders my love leave of its own accord. may that which blocks my circulation dissolve in this moment. may who-I-am-not run through this river back to the ocean. may who-I-am emerge clear as birth.*

she cried during the hours she was in there. she squatted, sweated, moaned. she bled and defecated and urinated and screamed. she scrubbed off layers of her skin. she pulled out most of her hair. and at some point she blacked out, exhausted. and the dark room held her.

the next morning when they came she looked rather like a baby bird. tufts of hair, raw skin, swollen eyes, dark red and naked. the midwives stung her with tea tree and she gasped. they wrapped her in cotton and she sighed. they sprayed a mist of jasmine over her and she knew.

she knew she could fly.[5]

most of us got there naked, burnt, raw with rashes, scarred. we had put down everything that didn't hold blood and some parts of us that did. we had brushed against the jagged histories that forced us to travel our different ways out.

television had taught us that teleportation would be all lights and a man in a unitard with a booth. that we would arrive wearing the same thing, with our organs and facial expressions intact. maybe one day.

our teleportation was slow and it completely rearranged us. we never put ourselves back together the same way again. it was a daily practice, slowly changing our sound from the inside, chanting and singing and listening deeper, moving in response to older harmonies than the reactive ones around.

do you know how long it takes to train hairs that would stand on end at any touch to become pores open with thanksgiving? it is slower than the speed of light but takes at least one candle every day. once upon a time the core of the earth made the magma solid, built crust around itself where dreams could safely plant and grow. we are of that lineage.

but in addition to the everyday, for each of us there was the one day. the one day we decided (or found out in the midst) that we were ready to drop every form of armor and be as vulnerable as the first teleportation, the day we were born. we believed our lungs could breathe a totally different substance. we believed our muscles would adapt to whatever measure of gravity or salt we faced. we believed that even if we were wrong in our beliefs we were right to believe them. it was the only thing to do.

and now we are here. as who we are. ready to scream again.[6]

they called them the air people. and they had their own mythology. they repeated the story of Igbo landing but they said it so fast and airy a lot of the children thought it was egrets landing. and they danced all the crane dances remembering their wings. the air people sang the memories of the people who could fly, but they got their designation from being *of* air, not always *in* the air, it was the way the air moved through them that was strange or necessary, depending on who you asked.

all those centuries of holding breath, policing the smell of breath, keeping a contract with death without honoring the preexisting one with life, made the air people necessary for us. beautiful and filled with light. sometimes when you saw them you thought you were seeing ghosts, but that was because the ancestors took immediately to the open and more open passageways of their songs, their porous limbs, their bodies that didn't seem to need to hold on to anything for long. they went to their natural extreme and like a dream you would meet them and remember everything and leave surrounded by whispered messages from your own dead and gone.[7]

soon she was shaped like a ghost. had it always been so? she had noticed that in crowded places people always seemed to find her to be the route of least resistance. there was space where she was standing. she was space for other people's journeys. no one could see all there was to her. it made her feel small. she poked her elbows out and broadened her shoulders. she wished she had a retractable fan that popped out of her vertebrae like a dinosaur. she wished she had huge angel wings to slap the faces of the unseeing everyone. nobody thought she was such a big deal.

or

wherever she was there was space and ancestors came through. they were drawn to her like they had been drawn to all the shores and like water they began to shape the stone of her back into sand. she recognized the shape of stardust. she breathed deeper to feel them moving. it didn't take long (only eternity) for the evidence in her side abdominals to show the work of breath, the depth of working. her movements became dance for landing light. her offering to the heaviness of heaven. she cultivated fluid-nuanced hips to stretch the follow-through of being. her bones decided not to know their limits. the space around her shone with beckoned peace.[8]

when the memories started to come back we were sleeping. not quite dreaming but regenerating our cells. almost dreaming that we were regenerating cells. on the verge of regenerating the cells that would let us dream deep enough to remember.

we didn't know about the liver cells that could sing. the stomach lining kaleidoscopes. the geometric worlds in our larynxes. we had explored our bodies like battlefields and colonies. never like fun-houses or arboretums. until our days became boardwalks on a rising sea and the nights we could sleep became worth saving, like named and labeled trees.

when the memories started to come, we were untrained. we didn't even know how to tell each other what was happening. eventually we would learn to share what went on while we were sleeping with all the specificity we had reserved for waking life. but at that time, when the memories came back, we were only starting to know.[9]

when they closed their eyes they saw rainbow spectrums at first. they
sorted through the colors like kaleidoscope workers. saw need in the
shaped refractions. they touched the spaces in need of cooling with
the soft backs of their hands. they kissed the places in need of heat-
ing. soon they could see murals and architecture when they closed
their eyes and held each other and they added to the artscape each
time. say it. you say it. say it. *you are mine.*[10]

then we cleared out the shelf space in our lungs. we dusted our convenient ribs. we trusted our muscular hearts. we tied ribbons all around inside. we laced them through our organs with no function but love. then we noticed that the only function of our organs was love. and we let them breathe again.

we took off our leaden clothes and we skipped out of our concrete shoes and we went barefoot enough to bear the rubble we had created just before. we let the sun touch us and felt what we had done to the ozone in our daze. we noticed that skin was just as thin as it should have been and all that we had been calling skin before were layers of accumulated scars.

we touched each other's hands and found them warm and ridged with remembering. we traced the lines and found home again and again. home was like a pulse. home was where the hurt was. we lunged and pressed towards each other's chests. we let longing lead long past our labored lack. we held each other's hands. they did not break.

we painted the walls with our breathing. we painted the walls with our breathing. we painted the walls with our breathing and found they were not walls at all. they were the forests of our forgetting, beautiful and dark with medicine. we marveled. at the patience of the trees.[11]

when they cut us down they found our layers, obvious as orbit. there was the year with the blood in the groundwater. there was the year of the sulfur in the sky. there was the year of bark turned blue with freezing (in the middle) in the middle of july. there was the time we focused on waiting. there was the time we warned them with lines. there was the season of not enough ozone and way too much sunshine.

when they cut us down they found us open to what they easily could have known if they had paid attention to any one of those seasons through which we had grown. we offered ourselves to their breathing. we offered ourselves to their homes. we offered ourselves to their dull admiration, their need for protection, their forehead intuition, the walks they walked thinking they were alone. we chipped into pieces to soften their playgrounds, we bent in strips to ferment their drink. we made every component of their housing except the kitchen sink.

we watched and grew thick with the knowing, we bent with the load of their love. it's not easy to be resilient when you feel from below and you see from above. we broke in the middle so often we thought we'd evolve past hearts. and we'd offer ourselves for release (but we want to see the next part).[12]

they called to her. the wind mothers. they wanted some new air. they deepened their breathing even though the toxins pained them. a guttural *ugh* on the in-breath, a forceful *yah* on the out. they started to dance-invite her. whirlwind of their cells, ancestry of their hips, opening out into song,

their arms made infinity.[13]

she puts her hands together and she is split whole. she is spit home. she is lightning through the middle leaving longing longer. she can reach. she is not static. just electric like the wires wiring money and time. like the towers that touch each other and say skype. like the satellite floating in the sky feeling more lost than anyone. she is praying without words. *may i conduct what is needed. may i construct what is needed. may i be known across the water without my name. like thunder far away.*[14]

there was a world made of her screaming. trade winds and thick-leaved plants to sustain the sound. there was only enough air for her screaming. nothing else.

as a planet formed out of the whirlwind, dirt holding itself together, water streaming through, everything was attuned to the howl. it became the most solid planet in her universe, that world made out of the scream.

how could she have known that aliens would come from all parts of her DNA to mine her pain like it was gold. how could she have known that a species would emerge and go extinct to the sound of her rage. how could she know a daughter would come along who wanted and needed the sweat and tears she flung off as by-products. never mind the salt.

there was a world made of her screaming. an ecosystem to support it. the solid place we stand on. the calcified weight of her screams.[15]

at some point she stopped counting the lifetimes. she knew they would recycle the names. or maybe the lifetimes became something like days of the week were in capitalist times. and knowing all of the languages just meant all the names meant the same thing. all the names meant "she is here." and they were wonderfully, fearfully spoken. she stopped needing numbers and names in order to know herself. they became arbitrary.

once she found her own eyes to look into, once she found a peaceful center to spin around, it was okay that time and language were as changing as air and water. you could pick something up and put it down anywhere. that's what she knew. and so the next time (or was it the time before?) when she was born again on the coast of west africa and spun screaming across the atlantic she made a song for the landing. *they cannot name me.* she sang in the languages of wind and DNA. *i come to take names. i come to break names apart.*[16]

Archive of Fire

Rate of Change

| H |
| Hydrogen |

| He |
| Helium |

| N |
| Nitrogen |

| Ne |
| Neon |

| Fe |
| Iron |

in the center of her chest, the fist-sized muscle was turning back to carbon again, burning black and then blacker like it wanted to be diamond. the scroll had said her heart would change, but she never imagined it meant this.

here, on the planet of sulfur and memories, she leaned her cracked back on the hot and broken ground. was this lava or her blood? volcano or revelation? what she was breathing would not have been called air. except that it was everywhere. except that she was breathing it.

there was never rain, but she waited for lightning to find her. the mercury of her veins aligning with the shock of being here after everything and before whatever. her heart was accelerated coal, growing deep dark and sharp. she kept on breathing, prostrate, burning, knowing soon it would be clear and unbreakable. her beautiful blackening heart.[1]

she didn't know she was waiting. she only knew she was breathing and her breathing shifted to the breathing of a being that knew something was moving, that something was coming closer and closer every day. so she waited. for what, she didn't know. could she say for whom? or was that just wishful thinking?

at some point she heard new voices. not known voices. not the voices she knew. the new unknown voices sounded frozen and far away and close and closer like breaking shells. they asked, *where are you?* and she said, *here.* but not with her mouth, just with her being. she said *here* repeated infinitely just by the fact of her being here.

at last she felt a contraction. and as she could not move and she could not see and she could not smell anything or have any real sense of what the sulfur was doing to her skin, or whether she had skin at all, she just stayed there. but that was the arrival. and without needing her long beat out eardrums they asked her the question. *have we made the crossing?* and that was when she knew. finally she could cry.[2]

at first nobody signed up for the courses, some knowing it would add them to surveillance lists, make it harder to fly, insert clicks into their phone conversations, make their windows more than windows. and some didn't need to know that, already having told themselves that freedom wasn't allowed specifically so they wouldn't have to ponder the consequences. but eventually they showed up with the only permitted writing utensil (the crayon) melting in their hands. soon enough they realized they would have to memorize everything, internalize all of it, keep it in their bodies. soon enough there would be nowhere else to keep anything anyway.

and the people watching eventually saw the patterns. they knew to watch for singing and the radiance vibrating off the skin of the student teachers. many felt so attracted they begged to go into deep cover to infiltrate the courses and each and every one was welcomed and converted. freedom is not a secret. it's a practice. it's contagious. the would-be infiltrators could not get the songs out of their skin. they could not resellout the places where they had internalized freedom. they could not undo the implications of the rituals they thought they were sneaking into. and that's how one at a time the watchers became the watched. the new attractors of their bewildered colleagues, pushed seemingly by their desire to crack the core, but actually it was their desire to access freedom.

people called it a cult and a misguided fad. stand-up comedians compared the sessions to key parties with swingers. even radicals dismissed it as just as hopeful and insufficient as 1970s feminist consciousness-raising groups. religious leaders just thought they were Baha'i. but eventually the curriculum was everywhere, transmitted between roommates and on buses with the tenderness of love. there were children showing up qualified to teach all the advanced courses. they needed bigger and bigger spaces, so they started to meet outside, and then they didn't need classrooms at all because the practices were jumping off everywhere. not without effort, but without force, all day through their eating and conversation. sometimes they stopped and marveled about how thoroughly they had replaced the story that was there before, but usually they just stayed in the practice and watched the world transform.[3]

if you treat it like a small and fragile light, vulnerable to wind and whatever, easily extinguished by the weight of our steps, then everything becomes a dance. you have to release the heaviness in your body and get gentle with darkness on the move.

those were her second instructions to the candle calisthenics class. the first instruction was *hush*.

they met in the woods at first, and later in basements. and no one knew they were walking around all day with their mantras. *breathing is burning and burning is beautiful*. they were learning to move as if the world was hot and melting. which it was. but this was no hot yoga trend. they recruited each other silently, new initiates following students to meetings of their own free will. not knowing that a *cinnamon* could only be perceived when she wanted to be perceived. and so each initiate chose and was chosen.

they were using candles to train with, but their real object was air, life, light. they were learning what heat and impermanence had been trying to teach our species since the first woman made friction into light to watch her sleeping selves.

they remembered each other through burns and breath training and no one left, so the contingent only grew. and they grew to know each other so silently that the partial movement of an eyelid, less than a blink, could lead them all in changing directions. they grew so quiet and so gentle they could hear each other's ancestors saying, *left here baby not right*. whole groups of them could move in stealth.

and so the second and third goals were achieved. both in service to the first.

2. develop the capacity to live underground, as close to the core of the earth as necessary
3. learn to move above ground and return undetected[4]

they became heated. more volatile. inside. and while everyone thought of global warming as an external phenomenon, it was happening on the same timeline within. the people on the planet were stars burning out. which explains the general urgency, most of the cancer, and the importance of the transubstantiative impact of dreams. something can turn to anything if you get it hot enough. we watched as the water in their bodies turned to steam.[5]

what we wanted was to want to. not to have to do anything. and the problem was we forgot after all these years of force what wanting was.

want was not getting, nor was it having. wanting was not needing. wanting was not having to have or needing not to need. it was not. and there was a wideness in wanting that didn't quite fold in on itself. it deepened and rose up and radiated out and touched softly to itself with warm warning.[6]

we ourselves made a world too hot for our feet and tried to teach our children to walk in it. we did that. we made the water flammable too. like we wanted to birth dragons, give back the planet to the dinosaurs, whose fossil fuels we fed to motor growling monsters. we told the universe in a million daily ways that we wanted to leave.

was that our warning? when we started to make shoes out of the same material as tires?

once upon a time they thought the end would come from above. so they trained their children to hide under the desks at school.
once upon a time they thought the danger was in buildings. so they trained the students and the workers to evacuate at the clanging moment of truth.

but actually the fire was always all through us. and there is no bunker to hide in. no way to get out.[7]

my teacher said the training explained it, but i knew it had to be more than that. we were not just running across hot coals, jumping through blazing rings, and juggling lit nunchucks anymore. we began to really breathe fire, instead of extinguishing it with the damper of our breathing. we learned to ignite all the oxygen within us, hydrogen too, without the pain we thought would come from blackening our lungs.

the acupuncturists said it was filtration, that we had evolved systems to parse out the carbon that we are. i guess we all had our ways of making sense of it.

but what i know is that before the change when i felt the ancestors near, like really knew they were here, it would always bring tears right to the surface, towards cooling peace. there was an inner rush to balance, to offer water to the spirits. our bodies hospitable crossroads, the water within us still available for the crossing.

and after the change the message was different. like the unseen didn't need a landing place, they wanted a spark. like the cosmic vehicle needed an ignition and we had made our bodies fossil fuels. so now when they show up we rise fevered and all our breathing says is burn.[8]

those were the ones that decided to steal themselves and donate each other back to the collective. drastically different in form, substance, and belief from the ones who sold their souls and bodies to the nonprofits.

the prophets had been saying the same thing for centuries, but when the point of the seattle space needle punctured the last oil refuge the vibration shifted enough that they could hear it. you may not be able to imagine it from here, but back then their very breaths were billable debt, owed back to the ones who wished they never had been born. the bodies of our mothers were land, owned by slumlords, burned to the ground so they could get the insurance money that would enable them to wait until the neighborhood was cheap enough for the speculative visionaries to take over with their student loan dreams. which is to say no one was free. no part of anywhere was free. something had to be done, but what could they do when everything had a price, if not on the stock exchange then in the ledger of their hurting hearts never feeling fully whole.

so they stole themselves, which was a break with everything, which was the most illegal act since the law that made them property, and they had to re-rhythm everything, re-tune bass in their chest, and immediately and perpetually they gave themselves away, the selves they had to give, the reclaimed flesh and bones and skin.[9]

the prison tattoo artists were ahead of the game. they knew without anyone having to spell it out that the body was the home that mattered. that matter was the muscle of home, no matter that this too, this very flesh, could be repossessed. well it did matter, and how much more important than the inked science of permanence, the reverence for becoming gods with the most beautiful talent for rebirthmarks.

so the people spelled out their names. the names of their crews. the names of their dead. they sketched the remembered symbols that fell out of their knocked-around heads. they drew out the lines in the faces they would never see again. they built room on their skin. and when even their skin was stolen they remembered the maps and went within.[10]

eventually they all remembered that they were their own great-great-great-great-grandmothers and they started to think of their grandmothers and mothers as more than the reason for all their neuroses and aggravating needs. they began to acknowledge their foremothers as the daughters they had always wanted to have. they started being, just being, the mothers they had always wanted to be. they remembered the selves they had sent across generations and realized it wasn't time that would make the difference, nor the specific mass of land, it was the act of choosing. of choosing each other. again.[11]

eventually the blankets wore thin and their knees and elbows pushed through their clothes until each little thread became filament and anyone could see how everything was made.

eventually all the glass was magnifying glass and they felt like they were living on microscope trays and god was somewhere analyzing the pathology. they were very conscious that all it would take was a certain angle of sun to fry them like ants and that angle was inevitable. not knowing when made them reckless in their trust and irresponsible in their love attempts.

all those threads fraying out of their threadbare clothes, which had been temporary and not high-count anyway, regardless of which designer's name had been prominently or discreetly stitched where, found another destiny the thinner they became. they became filamental micro-antennae to an invisible surrounding sound that whispered all the time instructions. the refrain being *close your eyes and listen*. let's see. let's see if they can close their eyes and listen before they get fully naked and burnt up.[12]

they looked each other in the eyes every time and did not leave each other without singing a prayer: the name or the wish. they learned to add touching hands into the ritual, a tradition newly sacred after the memory of the epidemic.

and of course none of that would have been possible if they didn't remember to look themselves in the eye every morning. or to chant the name of the prayer. or to track their dreams for keeping and sharing.

there is a sacredness to every day. every time.

it means again and again. it means all of us. it means this moment. this time. you and me. we're here.

which was something they would never again take for granted.[13]

Archive of Ocean

Origin

H
Hydrogen

O
Oxygen

Na
Sodium

Cl
Chlorine

this is what it takes to cool the planet. hold the world together. pro-
tect the mysteries (despite the surface violence. and the pollution
you try to bury in your heart).

this is what it takes. the strength of no separation. the bravery of
flow. the audacity of never saying this is me, this is not you. this is
mine, this is not yours. this is now, this was not ever before.

if you listen, each drop is saying always always. which is homonym
with right now right now. listen to the ocean let go and become one.
let go and remain depth. let go and just be everywhere. salt particles
aligned with the stars in the sky.[1]

only water and love. only peace and breath. she is emptying her bladder for the gods. her heart for the here after here. her mind for the moving moment. her lungs for pushing through.

she woke up on a planet with no land again. and all the leg strength she had built pushing her brain towards the sky, pushing the rock-hard reality down, standing up for this or that, was now for floating. in this water without salt shore. so much for buoyancy.

and even the salt within her pores pours out with the effort of balance. diluted by the fact. no land. just love. no anchor. just air. the weight of breath within her the heaviest heaven. her mind becoming clear, her heart becoming light.

and the light within is not the sun. her body not an island, but enough.[2]

and that was how we got the ocean. she thought of all the things this world could have been and wasn't and she wept and wept. all the animals and plants that never were, the people the people couldn't dream of being, the thoughts that would never ever occur to any of us so uselessly busy proving our lives away. she could see all of it. she could feel all of it. actually she couldn't see anything because she just kept crying, a heaving gasping cry. so her ragged lungs moved within the darkness.

crying laid out with no energy to get up or move an inch doesn't really look like the work of creation. but it is. it always was. salt, her face and all that never would be. she cried and it became the ocean. and out of the ocean came life as we know it. life as we be it. the salt in our veins. the who we are and the who we are not. we have not yet seen the bottom of it, the depth of mourning that birthed us here. and it was. well, it was. what it was.[3]

that was how the moon knew to pull the water or how the water knew to let itself be pulled. in this vast collection of tears there was more than jazz and tearing away. there was more than spit and amniotic memory. there was more than the liquid of it, there was also the heave, the sobbing momentum of it, that feeling that kept us contained and moving most of the time, like if we started crying we would never stop, like if we opened up we would drown, that was how the orbit made itself perpetual and the water continued to reach.[4]

remember when we met? underwater weightless and flowering. remember when we laced fingers or didn't based on tides or passing whales. remember how our breathing turned into what would support us and everything else in the thousand-mile radius of echo. and how our heartbeats were no different than this ocean pulled by moon?[5]

remember? remember that the whole planet was ocean. everywhere you've been. that desert valley was the bottom of the deep where something sentient used to swim. and every grain of sand and mineral and currently growing tree is breathing in the ghost of ocean, the infinite face of the deep. how do you think you know how to breathe and be pulled by the moon? and the ocean. she'll be back soon.[6]

the salt took everything out of her that the sun didn't want. and when she reached the shore the sand cut her in a million places. nothing about her was elastic or quenched or smooth. and technically, she was alive.

while she waited for something else to happen, she considered that maybe something was happening. like maybe the sand cuts were turning into gills and the scales of her dried-out skin were appropriate. she had a sense of herself one day soon, being able to breathe through her whole body. and then she passed out again.[7]

after and before carnival. causing carnival, there was a craving. a salt craving for a particular smell. no one talked about it. or explicitly associated the sweetness of saltfish with the memory of being packaged and preserved (barely) while crossing over. it was a memory too visceral for verbs. but it was there. and some people waited all year for it like a release and an excuse to fully sweat. some people had to fly home for it. some people tried to reproduce it in the cities of their escape. they had to have it. and if they didn't get it one way, they would find themselves still seeking it in blood or a fascination with the body fluids of the exact wrong people. (in bed with them wondering why. in fights with them wondering why. in basements seeking a sacrifice to quiet the craving.)

there aren't any words for it. no one can put it on their tongue to say *i need the memory of being brined meat for monsters to snack on. i need a closeness made from the opposite of love. i need the anonymity of abject arrival. give me the scent of jostled grief.* no one would say that. no one ever said that. but they did sometimes pack themselves into rooms with unknown fire codes and stay and sweat until they forgot everything else. they did press up against walls and corners with a secret hope of splintering. they did take to the streets for carnival dehydrated and sweating proving an endurance no one had any use for. they did fill the whole island with the creviced sweat of knowing, evaporating into the odor, the taste of survival.[8]

on the ships they had to listen another way. through the erratic heartbeat of being taken, of waking again and again to loss. through the shackled impossibility of body language, even if there had been light in the space. through and through the constructed darkness of the hold grating against their skin. (their skin, which was made for light.)

they learned each other through friction and bruising. they learned each other by shape, by the melding of their body fluids, by scent. they learned each other as the salt of looking back. waking again and again to loss. they learned each other by taste, the thickness of air for sobs, for screams, for passing out.

they began to sense the subtle differences between base respiration and life. between spirit and survival, and because the veil was thin they learned in their nostrils each other's ancestors, not by name, but by the changing rate of shaking, the raised bumps on skin and what the air did just then.

and when they disembarked. if they disembarked. when they were pushed out onto land, the kidnappers treated them like an undifferentiated mass. or a mass differentiated by market value. which was part of the violence and all of the lie.

but in another way, it was also true.

by that time they were none other than each other.[9]

even their bones would resist and crag the jaws of bulldozers wanting to be found. *if they didn't want to be seen again*, the diggers wondered, *then why would they bury themselves like art.* and indeed. why trace sankofa heart on the coffin with nails. why hold a shell in a skeletal hand. and those are the ones who chose land.

can you imagine what they are doing underwater. shackles braided now with coral. hearts the shape of scattered lungs.[10]

they used to say you could find god in the ocean. well. they used to say the devil was in the ocean, but we had to learn to inside-out their words like we were underwater already. we added in the bubbles of their airless flattened fears. remember they were the ones who were afraid of what the world being round would do to their two-dimensional souls. you could follow all their fear and get to freedom if you listened well. if you listened with a well of upside-downness.

and so in a way they were right. we did find god in the ocean. in what it took to adapt back to the ocean. in what sound of breathing in the open middle in the names for the gods we needed, in what was required of our shaking loves. we found god in the ocean, or the god of the ocean found us. or actually we found ourselves so melted and submerged in what we had done that we had to become deep.[11]

they made a pod of many colors. dolphin pod. pod of peas. they made it out of their ties to each other. they made it out of blood and indigo and dried it with the salt of their spit, sweat, and tears. and they lived there until it was shaped like them. but the shape kept changing. because they grew.[12]

it goes without saying that the dolphins had been preparing. and communicating with anyone who could tap into their frequency. if we could have only learned how to breathe. if we could have only listened with our whole brains. if we would have only sung to find each other. or taught ourselves to read the waves.

we started to wish our skin was thicker. our noses farther away from our mouths. we questioned the end point of evolution when we noticed it wasn't us.[13]

when she touched the map it moved. sand floating on water, exactly as fragile as the world. so real she could not lean on it without breaking it apart. it seemed proportionately correct. mostly blue and brown. but who would have gone to the trouble to make a geologically correct replica of a planet falling apart. complete with a magnet moon to keep the water in motion and holding on.

she would have loved to see the core of the model, but from any side the diameter was too thick. her arms were too short to reach through the atlantic or pacific representations.

for a moment, she had a strange thought. what if this really was a world, with tiny beings on it. and she (outside of it) could topple mountains, cause tsunamis, blow down civilizations. she laughed and the water rippled her reflection.

she decided not to touch the map again.[14]

she put her hand on the water and the water was flat. she put her face in the water and the water moved again. she reclaimed her breath and looked down into the water. hand touching underwater hand. face watching underwater breathing. and she wondered. who was it that really saw the mermaids first. the sailors or the slaves who were ourselves. who was it that really craved the muscled tails, the predators or the pregnant. and who is it here right now staring and wondering at my face. me or someone else. someone linked and synched as part of me, has been here living underwater all this time?[15]

For Phillis

what she needed was the heat. not the cute little desk in the portrait. not the windowed room looking out on Cambridge, not the white mother mistress to believe in her. what she needed was the heat, and without it she died. and it was the crossing that stole from her her own lungs. ocean miles away from the first heat that held her. knots in her chest ever tightened. her own breath forever linked to the oxygen tank of western inspiration. her Jesus like a breathing tube plugging her open nose. wherever she was she would have drunk knowledge like a whale. processed poetry with her rushing heart. wherever she was her every breath was made for prayer. and she was here. so this was what it looked like.[16]

her relationship to Africa lives in the part of her that is eight years old. that is seven years old. when did it start? her relationship to Africa lives in the part of her that doesn't know how long a year is or that it will one day be divided into seasons, at least three-fifths of which will make her sick. Africa is not her mother, but her relationship to Africa lives in the time machine of her body on the same reboot date as her relationship with her mother. i mean they ended at the same time.

restart. her relationship with her mother lives in the place behind her eyes where she saves headaches for later and pretends to be surprised by them. the place where she doesn't eat. the place where she has braces, where she braces. her relationship to Africa lives in the place in her mouth where she bleeds and grows soft callouses. the place in her mouth where she forgets how to speak the words her mother used to sing. she will learn every western language and not fill that soft red place.

her mother is not Africa. Africa is the place where she swam in the dark. no. Africa is the place before she screamed chained there in the dark. her memory of her mother is the truth that taught her shallower breaths would save her in that cold place that wet place where ever after it hurt to breathe. her mother is the warning that said use your brain to protect your heart. her mother is not that dark place she doesn't remember. her mother is not a ship. her name is not phillis. her name is her mother's name. her mother's name is a vessel she screams in alone and surrounded and chained. this is not helping.

her relationship to her mother is different. her relationship with her mistress is different from her relationship to her mother. her relationship with her mistress is bigger than her relationship to Africa. she would travel the ocean to see her. she would send her across the ocean (not) to free her. she would understand her words. her relationship with her partner is different from her relationship with her mother. she would never approve. she would never prove her love by finally getting it together. mother is the name of the one who can save you. mother is the name of the one who comes when you scream. mother is the name of the one who keeps you warm. where were you when the sun died?

okay stop. her mother is not god. her relationship to her mother is not Africa. her relationship to her mother is a ship in the angry ocean. her mother is not god. Jesus is not her mother. but she doesn't know yet. she doesn't know yet. she is eight years old. her relationship to Africa is three hundred years old. her relationship to breathing only thirty-four years old. brilliance is a respirator. all those smarts. how can she run her heart. how can she heal her lungs. when she dies the floor is wood again. and someone is screaming. mama.

restart.[17]

she stands at the portal again, breathing heavy through salt. *x* marks the back of her hands. all her dry cracked skin all star opening pores. she is never ready. but the person in front of her falls, the people behind her whipped open and trudging. through the door, onto the boat, into the belly, onto the deck, into the ocean again, hoping to find a different passage out next time.[18]

you cannot carry this in here, a voice said. and she knew it meant her gorgeous leather luggage filled with grief. and her recently polished, frequently restained vanity case of violences received and held like love notes. *but this is who I am*, she said. offering her matching identification, stamped with lies. *this is who I am*. she repeated, trusting the documentation that had gotten her through everything so far. and there was no answer except for her blood and her breathing, quick with the beat of how much she had paid already. except for her back stiff with how she could not could not turn back around. and so she stood there, at the border, with not so much as a plastic chair to support her detainment. with only her shiny suitcases as witness. packed completely full with gently rolled-up excuses. she stood there at the border. a line drawn in sand. and the desert blew itself around her. she stood there at the border while the tide advanced. she stood there. at the border. then she took a deep breath, pushed both empty hands forward, and swam.[19]

she found that the hardest time was before the release, the hor-
mones associated with the soon-to-contract womb, the lactation
memories reminding themselves they existed. the mammal thing.
what is the menstrual cycle of a whale? she found herself wondering
as she forced herself to breathe deeper and quiet the rising com-
plaints. she resumed the posture, forehead to the ground to remem-
ber the training, to remember the earth was holding her when it felt
like she was holding the earth. she cued the sound of ocean waves
and cried and cried and cried until she could breathe again. did a
whale ever feel like it was swimming in its own tears? she lay there
and dreamt of whales, or what she thought were whales, wailing at
each other until they could surface again.[20]

she opened the first door and closed it behind her without looking back. and the second one. and the third one. three layers of glass as she entered and protected the chamber at the same time. from outside it looked like one huge drop of water. (some said a stylized heavenly tear) transparent and diligently shined on the outside, graced by the perfect mix of salt, phytoplankton, and zooplankton inside so the glass stayed clean.

if she had learned to open her eyes underwater she would have been able to look out and see the whole community, the long horizon, the living places and the places beyond living now. but this was not about a chance to look through water at what she already knew was there. this was an initiation. an access point to perceiving what she had never been able to perceive before. what the elders could only gesture towards. what the power-hungry rightly feared.

if her training had not been enough. then this was it. if her training had been enough, then this was everything. she noted the taste of her breathing. this last moment of air.

then she entered the central chamber. floating cross-legged until all the bubbles left her. and when it happened she didn't wonder who else could hear it.

she sang out. she sang out like a whale.[21]

she returned to the surface again. eased through the barnacled peaks that had been mountains and before that—long before that—had been under the ocean like this. as she reached the skim and exhaled, she finally felt grateful for the time of depth. or as her people had pronounced it death or debt like depth, all the same thing. the snow that had capped these mountain peaks was now part of the ocean that held them on the melted planet, the perfect place to meditate on surface and depth, the perfect place to breathe.

and as she floated she could feel anything that had ever happened on this planet and accept it all. each water molecule connected to the stars. so she happened to remember the time of the surface people who had hated and manipulated depth in their vain attempt to escape death. how they had blown the peaks off of mountains like this to dig out the darkness they couldn't find in themselves. how they had blasted into the ground threatening all the underneath water to frack out the darkness they couldn't trust in themselves. the surface people, she inhaled and exhaled, who blew a hole in the sky as big as what they were unwilling to know. and the depth beings, embedded among them, continued to work on their breathing, continued to feel a persistent breakthrough on the skull parts they would have called forehead. the depth beings said a different prayer. and the surface people made it true with the heat of their anxious dailiness. *let the ocean reclaim all of this, let the sea rise and caress what is hers.*

her ancestors, the depth beings, changed forever by their love for the surface people. learned to breathe deeper and process the increasing complexity of air. the surface depth beings, the inevitable evolution of her ancestors with their interest in twoness. the surface, the depth. their skin as it blued and thickened from the sun and what they did to the air. their shape as it rounded and arched to accommodate their ground-focused eyes. she could see it. the useful shifts in the continents of cartilage, the curved regrouping of the remaining bones. the never again having to walk on land. she breathed and imagined how separate they must have felt. how rebellious they proved, trudging like the surface was solid. desperate to remember the liquid core of heat. how liberating it must have finally been, the obsolescence of feet.

before she took in all the air she would need to dive back down, she let herself experience the surface just a few minutes more. she was floating in always. her belly underwater, her blowhole saluting the sky.[22]

here the water is not salt-bearing. it is not blood-bearing. you will not float on spit for generations. this water will bury you clean, like it should.

here the waves do not break rocks for fun, do not dissolve the day to send a new one crashing onward. here the stillness is as deep as it wants to be. here the only movement is us.

here the oxygen in water is not screaming. here the o in h2o is not a sob. here the roundest molecules are breathing quite peacefully, like they chose the job.

here the water is not waiting to waste you. here the sun is not stripping your skin. this is the dark water of renewal. offering only one message:

begin.[23]

Baskets
(Possible Futures Yet to Be Woven)

hold water. mother weaver said as she walked up and down the rows. the students looped the grasses up and down and over and around. *a basket should be able to hold water.*

and some of them thought about how others in the camp called this woman a basket case. or called them basket cases for sitting here weaving with her as often as they could. the guards allowed it because it was supposedly therapeutic, but something else was going on in there.

moses was here mostly for the stories the basket weaver told. they passed the time. the focus required to loop and thread quieted the racing in her heart about where her people were right now and when would she see them and how could she find them. she had learned the first day that if she didn't focus she would stab herself under her own fingernails. that had been lesson enough. for her, the weaving sessions were a meditation. she tried not to imagine living without it. she was already living without everyone and everything she had known. she focused on weaving the pieces of straw and grass together like the teacher said *tighter.* tighter in the end than her "close-knit" community, she thought.

the stories were about the world. Grenada and the spice trees, the many people who had made baskets in their times. Charleston and the Combahee. Eastern Shore and the Northern Star. at night after weaving days she could see maps in her dreams of pieces of land connected by water. wet land blessed by the breathing and blood of rice growers, spice gleaners, cloth dyers, and of course basket weavers. she woke up with felt geographies different from what she had learned in school about solid land marked by lines drawn by propertied deciders. they had blindfolded her when they brought her to the camp, but she had heard the water, she could smell it even now.

out of her reverie of looping and threading and pulling tight she caught the eyes of mother weaver as she walked back through the captives with their slumped shoulders, the piles of grass beside them. *hold water.* the teacher said. *a basket that can hold water can also float.*

hold water. moses whispered. catching the rhythm as the teacher continued peacefully, below the listening range of the guards. *and if you can make a basket you can make a . . .*

boat! moses blinked and bit into the next piece of grass, and tried not to smile looking down. mother weaver turned her back to her as she went around the next row.

loop and thread and loop and thread and pull.[1]

baskets of no

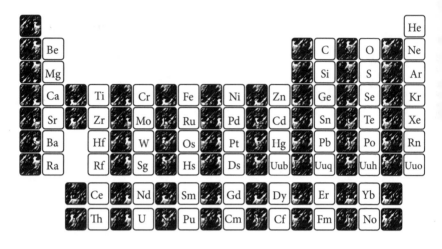

we broke the earth and now we fall through time. deep gashes in the ground. we scale the edges of our knowing. the smoother the worse, the more jagged the more better. what we stand on is not masonry. it is the torn place unhealed. the footholds come from how unclean the break.

we broke the earth and now we fall through time. because marching on a line we thought was forward only called up the urgency of the abyss. who said with her dilating presence *you cannot live like this cannot breathe the air here*. and so we witness layers. the ground time had buried over. awakened like the amber of escape. the fossilized texts we needed. landfilled manuscripts freeze-dried by the returning ice. we fell into the archive of our failure.

and this is what we found . . .[2]

you would look at me and you would want to scream until your voice went hoarse and you reached silence. you would touch me and want to cry the salt out so the emptiness could be real. you would taste me and want to run so far the sweat tracks no longer led anywhere. you would smell me and remember the end of dignity remember the filth that got us here. you would hear me and pretend that you could not.[3]

no one invented time. it's just that the sun and moon did what they did and we felt it. so no one had to abolish time either. it was just that we couldn't see the sky anymore and we didn't feel ourselves breathing. so whenever it was, we had no choice but to be present. some people believed that time was moving backward, which would have been nice, if it meant we could undo what we had done. or would have been just, if it was the universe's way of saying she wished we never had been born and was going to send us back to wherever we thought we came from to act so vile. we could barely find each other so there was no need to make appointments, not enough infrastructure left to require schedules, just the aftershock of being who we thought we were supposed to be until it broke everything. it was definitive, but like everything else (except for love) it was not always. so i do have to talk about it in the past tense.[4]

(when you said you loved me. and you lied.)

they asked her where flowers came from and she said: *the sky. there was something called rain. and it mixed with the sun. and they grew out of the ground, when the earth was brown. when the earth was brown like us and green. meaning ready and alive.*

they just looked at her. with no water in their eyes with which to cry. so she kept talking.

you put them in a glass. you cut them and you put them in a glass of water. and you arranged them so their faces faced out to face you. you put them in the middle of the table.

and she heard the youngest one whisper to the second youngest. *is it so you can watch them dying? or so they can look at you while they die?*

and the second oldest nudged the third oldest and said, *why did the people hate flowers?*

she took a breath. and started again. *no, the people loved flowers. they would get them for other people who they loved. they would give them as a present. they would grow them or find them or buy them to make the day brighter. they would give them on a birthday or if they were feeling extra love.*

and the children blinked at her and repeated it. *extra love. extralove?*

she went on. *they were everywhere. you could get them at the corner grocery.*

and the youngest interrupted. *what is a corner grocery?*

they would sell everything you needed. like food. and things you didn't need. like flowers and gifts.

and the second youngest said. *what is food?*[5]

there is compelled. and then there is compelled.

that was the other time we had gotten to the edge of everything. war had become the question impossible to answer and then the empty appeared with their swallowing want. (we didn't know.)

you have to know that we were shedding ourselves. you have to know that we felt alien in our hearts. you have to know that we already felt it. that never enoughness gnawing at our spirits. this is the only way we could have ignored the prophets and our own knowing for so long. you have to know how deeply we had given up, to trust ghosts to take you away. we lied and told ourselves that maybe across was a better place. and then we nailed ourselves to crosses here.

i don't have to tell you. but we were wrong.[6]

there came a time when they couldn't distinguish between them-
selves and the walls. they clocked through days to make enough
money to go home nights to sets of walls they paid for with those
same ticked, marked, and taken-over days. the luckiest among them
signed thirty-year mortgages when their lives were probably already
half over. they were the walls. they became the projected image the
walls sent out to earn their right to exist. which wasn't a right but a
privilege that lasted as long as the state didn't want to knock those
particular walls down.

and where did they send themselves to feed their necessary walls?
into other walled structures of making and doing and pretending to
know. the luckiest among them had built their own businesses out
of charisma and timing. they had signed papers bolting themselves
to those daytime drywall daydream treadmills that they had to keep
running in order to pay for the nightmare nighttime walls to be
there waiting.

they got experimental. they knocked internal walls down. changed
the cubicle to a workstation. went open concept. standing desk.
built tiny houses. rented collective basements. revived the revolu-
tionary building fund. crowdfunded crowded space for dreams to
live. commissioned graffiti muralists.

do you know what it feels like to love a wall with all your waking
days and dreaming nights? you will do anything to keep it. stay
when you should leave. bang your head at work. sign your very life
away.

so when everything imploded it was not the breaking bones and the
lost flesh that shocked them. everyone knows the human body is
fragile. what shocked them was how fast a wall could fall.[7]

it was not babel because the people had not built these towers to reach towards heaven. they simply wanted to unground themselves. to live on top of each other. to leave the planet altogether.

admit it. earth has always been a needy girlfriend. the type of woman who makes you feel obligated to show up and do stuff and handle her with care, just because she has been there for you when you didn't ask for it. you didn't ask for her to turn her whole life into space for you. and you can hear her. not asking but expecting. and ultimately she's too earthy. and really don't you want something shiny? don't you want the kind of woman who lets you enjoy the fantasy without having to worry about what happens behind the scenes?

it wasn't babel. it would be too much to make it as biblical as it was catastrophic. the fall was much more mundane. just the balding midlife crisis of the species. you know. the part where you turn your back on the mother of your children because you think you deserve better.

you don't.[8]

love. if you think you would have survived without the love of fat black women you are wrong. if you say it, you are lying. if you have blocked them out of your memory, it is because you do not want to know the meaning of necessary. you have failed them at the same moment you have failed the planet. which is every moment. say it. say the name of the fat black woman who processed your paperwork or fed you or cleaned something on which you would have slipped. say it before you die in your own filth. how dare you. how dare you say that fat means lazy and sloppy and wrong. who cleans? who works all the time while you are sleeping and hating yourself? who fixes everything you don't know how to do? you are a liar. you are a mess. and you are allowed to be a mess because of the unending work of fat black women. fat black women specifically. and you allow yourself to be a mess because you tell yourself. whoever you are. at least i'm not a fat black woman. even if you are a fat black woman. you've lied and said you weren't or compared yourself to someone else. it's failure. it's a lie from the devil. it will never work. it is killing us all. how many statues of fat black women do the ancients have to hide for you to dig up and understand what god looks like. how many times do fat black women have to save your life in song. what are you paying attention to? this is why you can never see god in yourself. you are damned by your hatred of fat black women. and no part of you could ever live without them. this is why the universe (huge, black, unfolding, expansive) shakes and shakes her head. you fools. you wasteful fools.[9]

this is how you prepare for a haunted planet. (on the scale of the galaxy they will call it a "ghost town.") you go to the city of the dancing funerals and the decorated graves and you listen. you walk around in the populated air and thicken your knowing. you breathe the backlogged water of the left for dead and smile a painted smile.

some people will tell you it's about sea level. but the sea doesn't have to level with you. it rises, runs at you, floods your footing. so those people are right. the bones of the drowned remain.

some people will tell you it's the exotic influence of the french. to which i say yes. something like that. it's that breathing funk surrounding every word. it's the throat forever trying not to gag.

some people will tell you it is an afro-indigenous holding pattern, a pact saying as long as you don't get it we will stay here hanging moss-like in the lingering trees.[10]

there was a certain numbness they cultivated without knowing it. not caring calcified in places they wouldn't have expected. an impulse they had allowed to flourish in order to protect themselves from the reckless energy of millions that surrounded them day in. day out. it began to build its own anthills against their spirits. and just like the city had routes and passageways variously under construction, their bodies became complicated networks of evasion. eventually they didn't know how they felt.

these are the things they tried in order to unblock the capillaries of being:

they tried drugs. prescribed and unprescribed. found and given. over the counter and over the top.
(mostly this exacerbated the distance)
they tried trips to mountains, oceans, lakes, canyons, and other sites advertised as "breathtaking"
(the effects were not lasting)
they tried yoga pilates hot yoga zumba jogging and other fitness-watch trackable activities
(while ability to endure feelinglessness increased, capacity to feel stayed negligible)
they tried the best food. raw, organic, fresh, local, pressed, vegan, macrobiotic, antioxidant, clean.
(it was as if the *not feeling* echoed in spaces cleared of fatty solids, some called it emptiness)
they tried the best food. imported. fusion. decadent. dripping. buttery. nostalgic. exquisite exquisite!
(it layered their organs. the lack of feeling bounced softly like if their lives were padded rooms populated by exhausted hazy strangers. themselves.)[11]

they used to scoop up everything we loved and put it in a machine. distill off all the excess. all the parts that could never be settled. all the parts that were older than history. all the parts where we loved each other enough to be completely afraid. the ecstatic parts. the purple parts. the parts with the racing hearts. and at the bottom of the process it looked like the state. it tasted like not much of anything. it was exactly the same process that made patties and fried chicken into the stuff of fast-food chains. and eventually the machine began to only feed itself and our duller tastes for existence. eventually they didn't even have to start with chicken to get us to show up and buy.[12]

remember when the people started to dress their children like cops? stitched blues defining their shoulders and bulletproof bulk to cross their hearts. you saw them on the playgrounds first. the children who had to get home by themselves at the end of the day. the only conclusion the parents could make from the dashcams and trial results was that to be protected by the police you had to dress the fragile part they thought they played. it was the last of the *see my child as human* strategies.

it didn't work.

but what a sight. younger and younger they got the navy hats and everything. and who would have thought they could make booties look like cop shoes? kids of color seamed and pressed with pins on their pockets. utility belts with candy bullets. they were children but they had heard the news announcers, they had read their parents' faces, they had lost their favorite siblings. they were not confused when they saw the smiles of the tall uniformed toddlers they emulated. they did not touch their pockets or reach their hands forward but sometimes their hearts jumped when they glimpsed themselves in glass.[13]

that was the challenge. to create oneself anew on a regular basis. it started with every seven years (also called the new cell cycle) and accelerated for the talented. to every three years, every year, every season, every month, every day until the prestige came from re-creating a self unrecognizable (to both your former self and the expectations of others) multiple times in any given day. they said it was towards the evolution of the community. a community that could not depend on previous expectations would have to evolve new needs. their individual shapeshifting was towards less collective dependence on a former world. *let the new world meet us faster where we are!* the people sometimes said to affirm a particularly brave reinvention.

they went from mostly not knowing their neighbors to perpetually not knowing themselves. which seemed more useful. and like the rare urban neighbor with the time to watch their transforming neighbors walk in and out their doors differently every day, the social media applications were even more useful for creating narrative out of the random moments of self-documentation offered by the digitally literate.

maybe that's where they went wrong. the watching. because at some point the point changed from transforming need and evolving skills to performing further and further newness. as if novelty itself was the measure and the outcome and the point again. and eventually it distilled down to the same people looking different every day and going to the same places they always went just to provoke contrast and doing the same things they always did (eventually just the work of looking for and financing new costumes). so the challenge was called off around the time when it got most boring.

it wasn't worth the use of fossil fuels.[14]

when we finally perfected teleportation it was great for a while. we could zoom to family functions and then sleep in our own beds. we didn't have "work travel" as an excuse not to buy groceries. we didn't have traffic as an excuse to not try some amazing food somewhere on the planet. it was the ultimate emissions save and not a moment too soon. (well . . . as you already know it was actually several decades too late, but still.) the mechanics started making gorgeous lightweight industrial art and no one could fight over oil and people had so much access to their time and each other. and maybe that was where it went wrong. or maybe it was a conspiracy involving the hotel industry. goodness knows the airline people had streamlined their profits with the building of ports in every neighborhood and in the cloistered homes of the rich.

maybe it was a conspiracy. but honestly I think it was just us. we realized, and pretty quickly, that no matter how fast we could get there, we were never where we wanted to be.

and soon all the blood it took to teleport didn't seem worth it. even if it was somebody else's. you know?[15]

the shortest way to say it is that they made themselves obsolete. the plushly educated learned to use the right words as cushions in their days. soft, soft, they suffocated meaning under diction. meaning it didn't matter. it was fluff they were training to be. how quickly could you find a right-sounding thing to say became the determining factor in interviews and semester-closing pleas to increase unearned grades. it was a skill that would serve them well as they negotiated their irrelevance in the next place and the next.

deep down they knew everything and kept it. protected it. which is why they were so nervous to be looked at. try it. look at them when they are silent. it's almost like it hurts to be so soft.[16]

the combination of digital knowability and pretend participation means that they agreed to it. the backroom deals didn't need back rooms any more. just distractions on twitter and petitions with broken links. when they got in the streets it was for photo ops. they mobilized to make the obvious visible, while the subtle deadly patterns kept moving.

there were the things they knew the president signed. and the things they never heard about. but they agreed to all of it, so thorough was their grief. so afraid were they of what they already understood. so nostalgic were they for a past they only thought was simpler because of the reductive way in which it had been taught. they were bought by the blankness they wanted in front of their eyes. they were anxious to ignore the beating in their hearts and the war drums everywhere.

there were the things they knew about themselves. and the things they refused to know. and they wouldn't grow. to take responsibility for their species, even one reflection at a time was too much. so they worked as if they were the fourth apprentices and not the master artists of their lives. they shaded and shadowed, at best they emphasized. at worst this is the paint by numbers they were always supposed to make anyway.

and so look. look what the world looks like now.[17]

they drew small squares in the dirt. with tape when they had it. with chalk later. and lime. white squares on brown earth. about a cubic foot. for sure no forty acres. this was how they plotted it. one cubic foot. enough to stand in but not lie down.

if you sat down, your knees might touch your neighbor. but you didn't sit down.

they got the idea from prisons, as usual. but they said it was biblical. *even pregnant mary and bewildered joseph had to travel to participate in the count*, they said. *you think you too good?* they said to the liberationists. *thought you wanted to stand and be counted.* even laughter tasted bitter those days.

the dirt-to-human ratio was disturbing. and that's if you take the record to be true. truth be told it was probably worse. but that was what it took to be part of the state. direct interpretation. *back to the roots*, they called it. fine if the supreme court had flagrantly ignored all the identity limits the seemingly white seemingly male ostensibly straight founding fuckers had assumed. the declarationists took it *back to the land*. and there you were. standing in your little box to be counted.

they started by stealing the meaning. out of everything you ever said. you let them co-opt the conversation you were having. with freedom.[18]

some people started memorizing phone numbers for the day when their phones wouldn't work. and they noticed the numbers they had memorized were people who lived nowhere near them. in some cases only the dead. and none of the numbers they knew were land-lines. they thought about it quite thoroughly in circles when they couldn't sleep.

it took quite a while for them to realize that on the day their phones wouldn't work the phones of the people they wanted to reach might not work either, and for the same exact reason.

maybe it was because their dependence on phones was total by that point. and the idea that their memories would outlast their devices was mere fantasy. perhaps they were not ready to remember what would really save their lives.

because after all of this, they still all thought of their situations as so very individual.[19]

one of us ran screaming from a plate with her open heart on it at the moment they said of our species there was nothing we would not eat eventually.

fragments of families fought their way through, backs tense and facing who they couldn't save and why exactly.

seven sisters escaped wearing white dresses hemmed in red that they didn't explain.

hundreds climbed silent up the highways, looking for more silence, or so it seemed.

many knew in their hearts that they had hurt the ones they loved. in the tightness in their lower backs they knew they loved the ones who had hurt them. in their brushing ankle reminders they knew they had chosen something more urgent than good. in our tired feet we knew there was nothing more to say.[20]

.

that was the strange part, when the signs disappeared. everything else seemed like organic karma to me up until then, devastating as it might have been, it matched the scientific outcome of our collective actions (and inactions). but i couldn't find anything to explain why all the municipal signs, the advertising signs, the metal signs describing the nature of streets, the neon signs radioactively saying open, the mundane signs just saying what a store was, the numbered signs on houses and mailboxes, were gone. and even if you could say why, i mean you could theorize why, in a world dominated by a species that ignored the obvious signs of its own decline and its arrogant approach to environmental incompatibility. you could even evangelize why with nuanced and blatant references to the tower of babel and whatnot (and people did, especially here in hong kong). you could talk about why the signs were gone, even if it had become much harder to meet up anywhere to talk about it. you could talk about it online for a while since the web addresses went last, but how could you explain how? as a scientist, as an engineer, i became obsessed with that part. the how.

could it have been a network of people coordinated enough to remove and hide the signs all around the world at the same time, but secretive enough that no one claimed to know any of them? did they intentionally leave the internet addresses up long enough for us to know that it was a global phenomenon and then take them down so we could not predictably think together about how to respond? was it a group of people at all or something larger? if it was a group of people, were they conscious of what they were doing? what if it was all of us? could we have taken down all the signs in our radius and then fully and completely forgotten what we had done? but if that was possible, wouldn't it have been equally possible that all the signs were still there and there was something inside us that wouldn't let us access them from here? (was there any "here"!!?) was there an element in the signs themselves that made them disappear? were we all transported, all of us, all the things we had made (except the signs), to another sign-less dimension?

to say that it was disorienting is to say nothing at all. the whole function of signs is to orient. but to not have any reasonable ideas as to how? i think it broke something in me forever. the time was fast approaching when i wouldn't be able to afford to care how the signs got lost, when i would even disdainfully appreciate the waterlogged and quickly illegible cardboard and paper replacements that people affixed. but i was never again able to trust that i knew the world i was living in or what i was capable of. i never really felt grounded in what i could see ever again after that. so that's why, for me, even though i lived so many years after that and witnessed too many other catastrophes, that was it for me. the loss of signs. that was the end.[21]

they say there was a time, in the womb or in prehistory, when the head and the heart were one organ, in one place, and the chambers of our being flowed together. and we have just been trying to get back there with humility and yoga. with bowing and stretching. with all sorts of remembered dignity.

sometimes it was more urgent as when the dancers leaned over and leapt at the same time, whipping their heads down and back up as if to invite the heart to elevate and the mind to deepen or to provoke an energy stream between the two.

and then there was the posture-breaking impact of the handheld digital device, training everyone's gaze downward and yes stretching the neck, and placing the forehead more directly in heart radius so the chakras could spark each other more frequently.

so maybe it was inevitable (that we would finally remember on the day things blew apart).[22]

there were stories about it. dating back from early. passed on by
elders. remembered in dreams. origin myths. at some point they
trained each other not to take them literally. and not being literal
or all that literary, they began to disappear. to seem to disappear. so
when it happened they were shocked. which shows that they were
not paying any attention to the stories they should have listened to.
they were spending all their time wrapped up in stories much less
true. or to say, more specifically, that the indigenous people, who
kept telling these stories, were so displaced and disenfranchised that
while they told the stories and while their grandchildren did listen,
the people who wanted to tear up the forests and frack down for oil
and build highways on the sacred mounds couldn't listen and steal
at the same time. or they could only listen enough to steal.

and anyway you can't blame the storytellers. because they did tell
the story and they even put it on the internet in a number of differ-
ent forms. and actually the truth didn't just live in the story. any one
of us could have sat on the ground and listened and known with-
out being told. the thing was we couldn't afford to know. we were
forced to clear land so we could turn it into money because we really
believed we couldn't live without money. but how did we think we
were going to live without land?

we didn't think about it. and some would say that not knowing the
stories didn't matter because how do you prepare for a huge event
like that anyway? but think about it. if you knew, really knew, the
implications of the weakness of a lawn. the cosmic uselessness of
grass, the real helpfulness of a diverse old-growth forest just in
terms of being able to hold on, the decisions about what to do with
land could have been completely different. and in the moment, in
the moment they could have at least sought an oak or another tree
with interconnected roots.

and really, if we had been living right, would it have happened at
all? i mean maybe it was all a response to the mining and blasting
and digging and polluting and paving and disrespecting. maybe if

we had known we would have been gentle enough keep the planet together. you know?

but anyway this is what happened. (and you can take it literally or not) one day, all at the same time, the continents got up, just stood right up after letting us live on their backs all that time. just stood up, gorgeous gigantic and brown and naked except for what we had built or allowed to remain. they just stood up and walked resolutely out into space. and the water between fell out of orbit and most of us fell too. unless we held on.

and the planet was gone.[23]

baskets of yes

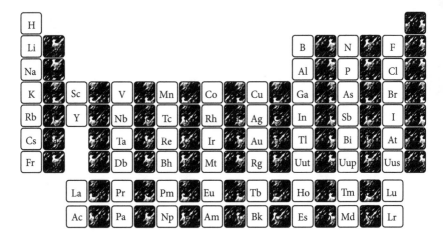

first we would have to say how they forgot.

they forgot because it was stolen. they forgot because they were stolen. they forgot because they were not us. they forgot that they were us. we forgot that they were us.

so that was first.

then we would have to say how we became a people. and then (third) we would have say how, as a people, we remembered. but we became a people by remembering. we remembered by becoming a people.

remembered what?
that you were a people?

that's what i was saying.
we remembered us.[24]

nobody celebrated or had a vigil the twentieth anniversary of the fall, the break, the breakdown, the breakup, the breakthrough. whatever you want to call it. why would they? the use of round numbers to provoke funding and attention was obsolete. no one was asking themselves or each other, *where were you when it happened?* because it finally didn't feel like everything terrible that had ever happened was about to happen again (prepare your body prepare your body), was up for renewal or wasn't over (prepare your mind your still-shocked mind)

if they celebrated it was because they had eaten. or because they had worked and needed to move it through their muscles before they slept. if they stayed up all night it was because there was a baby to cry with or a performance to think on or a decision to be hashed out the old way.

i know where i was though. twenty years after the fall. i had my arms around an oak tree. i was wailing, singing, screaming. i had my heart pressed to an oak tree. holding on.[25]

the space is woven. multicolored bright patterns lovingly threaded together. when you touch them, you know that each piece was worn by someone who believed in this quilted moment. this soft vibrant welcoming space.

and you can feel that the hands that stitched this together stitched it with love and desire, creativity and connection. they laughed sometimes when they were stitching and cried sometimes as the memories came though. they were grateful to transform each memory into love. you can feel their presence as you put the fabric on your hands. as you begin weaving now.[26]

that's why they made the quilts and ranked the pieces and kissed them and stitched them. they knew how to circle the cloth that had soaked up your sweat and salt into a map back to the ocean. they knew who was first and who would last and they stitched, all the while singing songs that let the threads too know their names. they were physical metaphysicians. they wanted you to be warm enough to remember.[27]

all of them moved. this was no coke commercial of people hold-
ing hands in a circle wearing costume references to the people we
had been. this was an oceanic embodiment. they undulated like
the skirts of the planet. they floated into the deep. it took a level of
aligned breathing usually only achieved during sleep. and when they
got to the part where they wound their waists into whirlpooled hips
and dips they were conjuring back the breathless wind of the death-
bringing angel-named ships. the only singing was the careful stars,
light breaking bonds in their shoulders. and the rhythm was rest
after rest teaching them what the sound was, precisely. what round
was. and that was how you found us. wasn't it? yes.[28]

before it broke it got thick, brittle, nervous, obsessed with itself and complete. silence made its presence unavoidable. most of us felt chapped by it, slapped by it. it stung. and no one sung, chanted, or marched when the worst of the deeds were done.

before it broke it got close to the ground that everyone needed to eat from and froze it or scorched it depending on what hemisphere you were in at the time. the people tried to divine but the shells broke in their bitten hands. silence became sharp as sand right as it turns to glass.

before it broke, it broke many of the people we know. whole families too hurt and proud to grow. whole neighborhoods too shocked to show themselves to each other at all.

for it to break, it had to fall from such a great height that no one was above it, not even the hoarders in their bunkers below. who shook and fell on the core-heated ground. all face down. (so the message came through.)[29]

some people said they had felt it in early twenty-first-century New York City after the financial towers fell for the first time. but that wasn't it. that was the false feeling of being "American" which didn't even include all American citizens. not even then. especially not then. some Black artists in the twentieth century had claimed a feeling of global citizenship when they fled to Europe in the early part of the century. it was short lived. some Black activists had felt it when they fled to Africa in the second part of the twentieth century, but their feeling of being human was relative and fed by enduring imperialism externalized. don't count that.

there did come a moment when the species was united on the planet as human, but it was not what anyone had dreamt. and it was too late to truly benefit those of us who had been called alien. we who had nonconsensually generated the human across time. it was what the Black speculative feminists called "the Butlerian moment." the more musical among them said "Octavian Overture." that moment when it was time to leave. when the true others finally arrived.[30]

they used to say you got to choose your parents from a viewing room in the sky. children have even been known to admit it. *i chose you so i could challenge you. i chose you to help you get this lesson. i chose you to teach you how much you could love.* but now, the bigger question is, why would anyone choose to come to this planet right now. to breathe fire and walk the broken soil. to be thirsty and lead-poisoned. to live like nemesis to the sun. to live through the revenge of the wind.

there used to be a story about a son named jesus. and how he came to pay a debt, to live a sacrifice, how he came with superpowers to die from the predictable betrayals of the many. but now they have stopped telling that story because that could be the name of any child. we look at them and swallow guilt with wonder. *why would you come to this forsaken place?*

(i came to teach you something else for goodness sake.)[31]

it was like that the last day we left the schools. all song. so many songs of the erstwhile schoolchildren freed and the generations crescendo-ing to meet us.

there was a time when no one would have ever thought there could be school abolition. except the sneaky privatization schemes that sought to destroy the students while keeping the buildings as monuments to how deep their theft could go.

it was the mothers who said it first. how total prison was. how the problem was not only their children being pushed out of school and into camps, but how the children drinking private school kool-aid were pipelined to more colorful camps. matriculating with programmed responses, like drones to kill the willing once they were made.

and the midlife crisis set who protested all the barbed wire put on their years as if learning was temporary. and what did they know?

ultimately it was the natural consequence of all our industrious work to make the air unbreathable, the water undrinkable, and the people uncritically unthinkable. at some point we needed all the different ages to solve all the problems we had excel-sheeted and databased into our lives.

so we abolished schools and prisons the same day. and the people came home singing and welcomed with song. what a noise. what a noise for every age.[32]

it was the ones who had been doing and doing and doing and going and going and going and going. it was the ones who refused to be undone by non-acting-loud-speaking representatives.

in my time we would have called the doers the black women and everyone else, respectively. understand that it was neither biological nor intrinsically attached to gender. there was a reason for the pattern though. the ones who did and did and did and went and went and went vs. the ones who never acknowledged that going and doing, and only acknowledged the circles they talked around themselves.

so the ones who had been doing the doing and going to get the going going got tired. but they kept going and going and doing and doing. (while the other ones talked about what they were going *to* do). and as the planet got hotter and more full the goers and doers worried about what would happen if they stopped. they took extra shifts when they should have been sleeping because when they closed their eyes they saw slideshows of catastrophic pictures under the headline "THE GOERS AND DOERS DONE GONE!"

no one else besides the goers and doers could imagine a headline like that, and if the goers and doers joined the lovers and leavers and just left, the non-acting representatives still wouldn't have acknowledged who had always been doing the going and the doing. it was an unhelpful fantasy of the get done group to think that if they ever stopped doing all the doing they were doing the others would see. (they would finally see!) nope.

you see, that would imply that deep down it was the doing of the doers that kept the talkers not seeing, which was not so. this was a grave misunderstanding on the part of the doers. they believed in the contingent autoimmunity of their own power. which is to say creation and destruction were mixed up in their guts and they didn't know any other way to deal with that except to go and do and do and go. do you follow?

but that was before. i am trying to describe to you what it was like when the doers decided to rest. when they carefully placed what they knew in the easiest places to find it and sat down. i don't know if wind systems really take deep breaths on their own, but it felt like it. the stillness was profound. and for a while all the talkers could hear were their own voices resounding like always, but pretty soon they had to listen for the source of this strange silence where the rhythm of other people's doing had been. it was the sound of a voice bouncing with nothing to take credit for. nothing left, finally, to steal. it was hollow and horrifying from that perspective.

and the former doers retained their restraint. some of them shaking in their seats. some of them repeating mantras and biting the insides of their cheeks, but quite a few of them just honestly passed out in the deeply earned and dreamless sleep of the overused.

you should have been there. you had to be there to really feel the contrast. all that frantic energy, all that back-and-forth friction and the robust remarking that tried to drown it all out. and then the moment it just stopped. and if it was truth you wanted, you could find it on the floor, in the kitchen, lying on the street just so. if it was truth you wanted, here it was. i mean make yourself at home already.[33]

when they watched human history like a silent movie, there was a group they called the reaching-hands-women. the brown women with hair like shock around their highly electrified brains. those who could read radiance looking back could see the charts they made during everyday talk and special conversations. like in Nassau when the witches gathered making a cauldron of themselves to speak their dreams. one of them stood up and started pulling stars out of the air down to bright them up, pulling whole moments of the past into the room so they could be shredded. she dug up so many bones out of the mud that she had to stack them very carefully on the legs of the women sitting around her. if you could look back and see the colors and combustions of all those reaching-hands-women who cared what time it was, and let time forget itself, if you could look back and see them, you would know that they reached for us. if you could see them you would know. we were born that day.[34]

we could always see through our belly buttons. we just didn't know what seeing really was before then. we depended on the periscopes in our heads to warn us, to show us, to teach us the good. we walked in the world like defense towers, but that wasn't the real shape at all.

remember when that person you trusted more than you trusted yourself told you to trust your own gut? the brain below your belly button that was always right? always right underneath the words? where do you think she got her info?

it was the half-blind poets and the beautiful remaining grand-mothers who finally taught us to see. to remember. to be.[35]

some people were afraid of the men who could give birth. what could they not do, these men who had raised themselves, daily becoming the men of their own dreams. how did they refuse their mothers? how did they become their mothers, these men who were not afraid to be pregnant or free. call it the end of outsourced labor. call it whatever you want to call it. it was miraculous every time.

some people were afraid of the women who loved black women. who loved themselves into black women. who styled themselves carefully out of rope and hope and curve. some people tried to tear down and bruise the beautiful ones. to perpetually delay their sacred work. the scarce ones begged them to forsake their destiny for paltry and pressed-down privileges. they used words like *unnatural* and *not real*. but what could be more natural? what could be more real than a person shaping herself in the image of god?[36]

they studied the differences between the words *continuous, continual,* and *constant* by writing them in sand on the beach. *every moment less land* their parents whispered where they thought they couldn't hear. they were raised to believe they could only trust words. words were a place to stand. even though they could be washed away. so they memorized the words in the poems they made for each other and they measured their presence in each other's lives. which was continuous before the demands of eating scattered them, and then continual when they returned like racing boats. but afterward, everything had changed and there they were with their gray hair and their remembered poems, their eyelashes attuned to how quickly the world can shed itself. and then they thought about the love and called it constant.[37]

their basements were not so much about keeping. i mean, look, the cluttered mantles and end tables. look the bright family pictures layered on top the older family pictures mailed year after year all crowded in the same frame. look how the whole place become an altar to looking well. pose and posture and figurines and cookie tins and evidence of other empires to leverage out the one we living in. it smells like we cooking a particular form of magic. and not everyone can cross this threshold. see where we place the mirror so you can see yourself out if you come with malice. no one saying obeah, but no one saying feng shui either. we have much, but we don't have much to put away. and really we used to living at sea level properly. or in rented rooms temporarily. or if is what they call "extra space," soon enough some cousin in there sleeping.

so basement is not a thing we really study like how you study it. or say basement is not a place where we put things we want to keep and ignore. but in some houses, and you only know if you should know, deep in the house is a place of blood and transformation, shells and seeds and knowing. a place of remembering and washing. a place of guidance and entrancement. and only the brave would dream to sleep there. but who know more duppy than we. they out duppy duppy in the basement, deep in the backyard, in the off-display places at home. living room is like the jewelry. layered and loud with performance. what you call the basement, we would call the heart. where blood run thick.[38]

the people who had been dancing in circles. charting the way back. opening their bodies to be inhabited by the elements. you can say they had an advantage. or that their africanness foreshadowed everything, just as it had overshadowed everything before the end.

their yellow and green meant they could predict a world. their yoruba and akan meant they could feel a world coming. which is different from preparation. they didn't prepare. they practiced. they played. the difference is important.[39]

and nothing else. they used the remaining drinkable water and everything green they could find to purify themselves from the inside out. they began to identify with fruit after they had redefined their understanding of fruit, distilled it down to its last and urgent function. simply put, fruit was a vessel for clean water. and so they needed fruit. and they themselves. to hear them tell it, they were vessels for the pure rage of spirit. or they would be. and so they were necessary.[40]

they used wax. crayons across the paper on the floor and one of
the last remaining record collections. they drew what they could
remember in color. using sound to reach back because the world
didn't smell like itself anymore. the oldest among them remembered
landscapes of grass and drew flat and rolling greens from where they
sat. and the younger the people got they more they remembered
brown, and then more orange and then red. the planet itself had
to signal STOP in their symbolic codes. but by that time, what else
could they do?

i like the footprints that the little ones tracked across the remem-
bered outlines of where there used to be pipes. where the gas lines
tracked through the cities. where the books had been held.

let's shape our new home in the contour of the last toddler foot-
prints. in honor of the ones who walked away.[41]

Memory Drive

Na	Mg
Sodium	Magnesium

K	Ca
Potassium	Calcium

Fe
Iron

Zn
Zinc

P	S
Phosphorous	Sulfur

there was the face she made when she pretended to be listening
there was the face she made out of papier-mâché
there was the face she drew on with pencils and painted with brushes
to keep the compliments coming and the questions away
there was the expectant three-year-old face she avoided
there was the face she anointed unceasingly with tears
there was the face made from pushing her mouth closed and biting
her tongue
there was the face bruised from falling down the ladder and hitting
every rung
there was the face that looked too much like her father and too
much like her mother and too much like her fear
there were the faces that went in and out of fashion every year
there was the face that faced itself and screamed and screamed
there was the face she thought was hers when she saw it in her
dreams
there was the face she felt for each morning when she rose
there was the exact same face but with a much longer nose

each face had its own neck
its own flex for avoiding sun
hydrahuge and hiding

and there was the sword
in her hand[1]

she had a self-sharpening spirit. that's how she would describe it afterward. everything that happened rubbed against her right in the middle until you could see her glint when she smiled. strategy-sharpened heart, what did she used to say? she could cut through the nonsense. sense-sharpened memory, she forgave immediately and never ever forgot how hot metal cut so much better than cold.[2]

she wouldn't tell us anything until we stopped knowing. stopped thinking that we knew, which came at the long edge of a lot of time spent acting like we knew. and then pretending to know what we didn't know. and then pretending not to know that we didn't know. she waited. she saw through all of it. at least fifteen times we thought we were ready. we thought we had let go of everything. we thought we were meditating right then in the midst of our thoughts. and she could hear it. every piece of held-onto knowledge clanging in our brains. every muscle memory of do right. so she waited through our impatience. our protest. our feigned indifference. she waited. and when it was over and all there was left was the sound of us not knowing nothing, then she began. and she said:

it all started when i stopped knowing. before that they wouldn't tell me anything... [3]

all the names changed. it was a long time people had been changing names. taking on aliases to escape, changing their names to freeman to let you know, or renouncing slave names by choosing swahili or yoruba ones on brightly colored days, or the letter *x* as landing pad for confrontation. or on the other hand some people had been through a process of name-whitening on voluntary arrival, so their names could fit in the mouths of the unwelcoming, so they wouldn't have to suffer garbled prayers at school at work at every adminis-trative encounter. and then there was the sex and drama that caused people to add or remove letters from their names because they didn't want to be associated with their fathers.

this was different from that.

all along people had been collecting spirit names through initia-tion. more prayers to layer over the prayers of their parents. more languages to pray in. more ancestors to invite. so when the change happened where the spirit world took back over in the realm of the embodied, all the names had to change. it was quite pentecostal. the people called each other out in languages they had never known. and they called them by the names of their deepest desires, their necessary evolutions, their soon-to-be-vanquished fears.

my name, at that time, right after the change, started with an *m* sound. i can still feel it. it was *move* it was *more* it was *maybe not messiah* it was *miracle* it was *moon*. it was many things in the lan-guage we forgot.[4]

the hyphens stopped working for them. soon after, so did the re-
claimed words in older languages. who they were was less place and
more time. or who they became were places moving through time
instead of evidence of a particular moment compelled across space.
maybe it was because no one wanted to mention their particu-
lar boat. or because as the state eroded it became less important to
claim a reconstituted citizenship.

the names for generations became important to the "millennials"
because they had more ways and faster ways to say their names
more times. but the gaps became smaller. soon, even siblings were
of different generations, their life spans shorter than the runs of
most on-demand TV series. they began to name themselves by what
they had witnessed. which horrifying moment had been the first to
keep them up twenty-four hours looking at twitter, CNN, and the de-
scendants of twitter and CNN. my teacher was of the ferguson mo-
ment. her teacher was of the moment of the superdome and flood.
her teacher was of the towers falling. i was of the moment when the
silence broke forever.[5]

she was always watching. even when she only knew a word or two, they could tell. she would mimic the movements, the praise songs, tone out the oriki in baby talk. so she knew. later, when none of those basements existed anymore, and the people that had known were scattered back into sand, she kept what she knew lower than consciousness, somewhere in the muscle memory, triggered at odd times by cologne or cornstarch or the right set of sounds in the right order.

the gods becoming human. she had seen it before. so she knew it was possible, even if she didn't know she remembered. even if she didn't remember knowing. you know what i mean. so later, they thought that might have been part of the reason.[6]

they heard her suck her breath in. almost whistling as she wrote the symbols in their palms. her tongue behind her teeth like an exasperated mother. this was the last chance. their palms would activate, or they wouldn't. the salve would flow through or not. she didn't give them the medicine because they were worthy or because they had worked hard. certainly not because they had been able to pay her to do it. she gave it to them because her hands could only reach so far at this point and something had to happen. she didn't end with her usual speech about the next ninety days. she didn't warn them to be careful until their new powers came into balance with the rest of their beings. she didn't think they had ninety days or any balance in their futures. she attuned them on the chance she might be wrong.[7]

she built it out of scraps she found on the road. the rubber of blown-out tires. the dented metal memories of how fast everything used to move. almost as if it had all wanted to rush to the end. wanted to break. she thought of caddis flies as she added piece to piece welded by her intention, the heat, and the pressure of the space between stones where she worked. marooned to the task of trying to put things back together in a different relationship than they had ever had before. the task of believing there was some possible relation that wouldn't mean detonation.

the point was that it was light enough for her to move and heavy enough to hold her down when the winds came. the purpose was that the light could come through but no one could see her in the dark. the major saving grace was that no one was looking for something like this in the form she had formed out of brokenness. it was lack of recognition, once again, that allowed her to create this small world.[8]

when she got there it was full. of people who left home never wanting to leave. of people never having been home on account of bank accounts below basic solvency. of people who made home for other people for pay. of people who made home out of their bodies for free every day. and the people who held those people's hands. and the people who followed those people having no better sign. as she moved through the crowd no one recognized her. it was clear that in the need to flock somewhere, to have some collective space and safety, things had happened quickly, mostly instinctively. no one had read her carefully worded manifesto.[9]

she wanted be like chlorophyll on a brown planet already too near to sun. she wanted to turn light into food and bright up everyone she knew. had known.

if i was the queen of the universe, she said to herself, *if i won the lotto*, she said, but didn't ever play, *if i came into some money*, but the amount of money they give you for being a genius (best-case scenario) is only enough to isolate you from the people you need. she threw her hands up. she had forgotten again. it was past that time. past the time of queens and only one universe and the dreams that had fed the lotto machines for so long and the foundation awards that let the children of slaveholders hold on to their money. it was the time of the brown planet and there weren't that many people left. she may as well have been queen of the universe by default.

what would you do? she muttered to herself thirsty and almost to where she thought home would have been. *what would you do?* dusty daughter of so many miracles all of which had led to this dry moment of wanting to be green. wanting to make light into food and time into water. and then either it was there. or it was an illusion. home had so often looked like an oasis. either she was there now and it was real or it had never been real and she had lived in a projection of well-watered life the whole time. she thought she had reached and she sat down with no tears to cry, no words to say, just the dry light of being. and she knew, she was only and ever and always and only her prayer.[10]

what her hands could carry was a good question at this point. with the nerve damage and arthritis. with the dryness and the healing fatigue. what could those hands which had done so much laying on carry now? sometimes in her dreams she would imagine she could hold a pen and write and write for days and when she woke up she would cry and curse her hands and how they had been changed by all the tapping the typing the type to click the swiping and scrolling. they had truly become different organs. would her grandmother recognize her hands? if a baby were to be born could these hands catch, could these hands cuddle? she sat still and prayed, hands open on her knees like the peaceful new agers of the old times. it hurt too much to clasp them at her heart.[11]

she put her hands out again. another digital misread. what nail-biting and friction had done to her fingertips was no joke and the print recognition technology was not laughing. she took a deep breath and placed her hands gently, two at a time, on each face of the hexagon of mirrors around her. each time looking directly in her own eyes as if to say, *it's me. it's me. what this world has done to my hands has not destroyed me.* on the sixth placement there were tears welling up. recognition is no joke. she sniffled. *who's there?* the computerized voice asked. again.[12]

dreams will get through. even if you stopper up your mouth and tighten up your behind. you are not airtight. however shallow you make your breathing, the depth is there.

the old woman snapped at her as if she had seen the dream where she was a boat and a boatbuilder layering and layering herself over with wood. or the one where she was a serpent, shedding skin to find less porous skin and failing. or the one where she was a palm tree always reaching up only to fall out and more out with each generation.

but she sat there with her legs crossed and with two hands over her open mouth.
tense and horrified.

she didn't know she was ready.[13]

when she sat still and looked at water or a mirror, she could remem-
ber. or, to be more precise, she was aware of her function as a tech-
nology for remembering. specifically, she activated her body as a
connection site for all intergenerational knowing and reveled in
the edges of herself. looked in her eyes and laughed without sound
at the transparency of the processer she was. sometimes for a mo-
ment. sometimes for the length of a jazz song. sometimes all morn-
ing long.

(other times when she was in response mode to the many she just
remembered the sound behind the letter *y* as in *yay* or *yikes* or
yesterday.)[14]

not being one. not being even only two, jagged across time, she stretched. and it seemed like all the space she opened would be filled with tears and ships and screaming mothers. but she kept breathing, remembering the impermanence prayer. and her muscles expanded enough to embrace not the pain. the pain she simply witnessed with the wetness of her eyes, the evacuation of her brain as she blew her nose in tissues. she embraced the greater clarity of all the words that bottleship pricked her at all her unfortressed corners. this was this. this was not the time to speak.[15]

she was learning to wait. she was trying to learn to wait. "hold up" was that space in front of her chest as she moved towards a person, knowing she would rather be holed up in her room reading maps. so she made a miracle-stitch of pockets and dropped heart oil and crystals into them. sometimes she could read their hearts from ten feet away. she put the magic in her hands and breathed forward.[16]

at that point mirrors became dangerous. puddles were treacherous. windows weren't windows anymore. they were doors out to inside. wherever she was walking, standing, sleeping, sitting she could see a portal. she felt too portable. where to look?

but after days of seeking out matte and stucco surfaces to rest her restless eyes she gave up. she sat on the floor with a bowl of water in her lap. and said, *fine then. tell me.*[17]

it got so she could see them with the slightest refraction. any puddle of remaining water or spilled oil. glass, plastic, and what came after. the glint of sand. only while moving. and only out of the corner of her eye. she could see her sisters.

part of her knew they were always there. part of her longed to look at them head on in stillness. sometimes she wondered whether her nearsightedness helped or hindered the connection. she began to track them as she moved across alone. *there*. she would say. trying not to change the angle of her face. *there*. the glimpse of hair. *there*. *there*.

what ultimately saved her was the listening. because while fleeting, it lingered a little longer. like a kiss on the cheek. at first that's all it was in fact. unpredictable kisses out of nowhere and laughter accompanying the winks of glass and edge. and then she would hear small affirmations. and then repetitions and sometimes even jokes. there were so many of them. and they were so light and quick to surround.

so that day, when nothing else could have helped her. and when she had given up on being able to help herself or anyone else. she called them in. *sisters of glint and glare, sisters of whisper and wind. i need you now.*

i need you.[18]

speak life.

that was the only instruction they gave her. and her throat scratched
with it. her forehead pulsed too bright with it. her gut fluttered. she
told herself she was not ready.
she decided to sit at the machine and try to learn every language,
desperate to find one old enough to ring true. what were the lan-
guages left to listen in? how could she know?
drawing in the dust of screens and keyboards she had the thought.
what if what she was here to say was something no one had ever said
before. something that no one was listening for and at the same time
the only thing she could say.

so at some point (call it the seventh day) she decided to let it be.[19]

she sat still because she didn't hear anyone calling her. she slept and dreamt again. and she awoke to the silence with the memory of a demanding voice. *when are you gonna give ME a gift? what is the wrong answer? where is the inside?*

she still sat because she didn't know how to spell her name or that her name was the spell that was making this happen. and she waited and she waited and she waited.

and when she got up and walked she thought it was the soreness in her legs. an overdue need to stretch. she thought it was a giving up.

but in fact it was her answering the way that every tendon and muscle had been breathlessly screaming her home.[20]

that was when she learned to stretch. she nurtured the tense inten-
tion to outgrow her skin. to reach for what was nowhere nearby. to
embrace the unembraceable around her. she let her fingernails grow
out, refused to trim her edges. she wanted up through the ceiling,
down through the floor. she refused the short limits of this body. she
wanted to be long.[21]

it was in her thighs. she felt it in her thighs. all the hardening all the strength all the muscles made for making it through all the never-loosed let gos. it was in the lining of her stomach. the poisons she drank in carefully labeled jars at manageable doses. not her broken heart. not her shaking hands. it was in her thighs. the fear of what it would mean to bring life here to allow life through. she was the carrier of the old decision from the slave days. no birth till we get home. no babies offered to the monsters. only monthly blood offered to the gods. she can feel the moon watching her and telling her the time has passed and home didn't stay where it was anyway. she can hear the ocean tinkle bones at the bottom that say maybe maybe somehow.

seven generations ago there was a woman who loved her. who was her. and she broke the vow. she broke it in celebration and she is screaming now now now now now.[22]

she taught them about shoulders. how upside down, they could still carry the world. she taught them about air and how one way to get it is to scream. she taught them about breathing and that the first way to do it is underwater. she taught them about the necessity of lubrication, the bright beauty of blood, the elasticity of membrane, the flexibility of a body holding on to itself, the grace of a first dive.

and she would continue to teach them so many things. simply by being alive.[23]

there she was beaded to the wrists of strangers who looked golden and languid who looked to her like images made from plant and sea glass who looked to her like the promise of the sun fulfilled. *what had they done to regain the original dignity?* and why were they contained to only one island on this big planet.

the oracle shifted her hips. grooving back into embodiment as she landed. it was as she had suspected. dignity itself (the other spelling of her name) had been internationally outlawed and confined to small island spaces without bridges. spaces where she was shamelessly loved in green and gold. she smiled a mouth full of shells. (eight above, eight below) and joined the dance.

she was back to do her work.[24]

first she cleanses. scrubbing everything that is not her off her skin, out of her hair (like the planet does, she thinks, like the planet does). she steams the air with new wet oxygen so she can exhale all she needs to exhale (with gratitude to the trees) and then she burns up all the breathing she just did (with oils and sage and candles).

and then she starts.

she imagines electrons sparking (*eji ogbe*, she says, *let there be light*) and she encases them in a wild orbit around atoms (*and let there be darkness, my love*) and she differentiates the molecules (*see to it, see to it*) and sets them all on their tasks. and finally she yawns and screams.
finally she laughs and sings.
sound the alarm! I am here![25]

i knew the ones who would understand wouldn't be here for three thousand years. or three thousand minutes. or three thousand seconds. or three thousand days. or later today in the year three thousand. truth be told i didn't have much use for the specificity of time in there. and i didn't think i would keep existing for any unit of time.

what i knew was that the ones who would understand were not here now.

and so i decided to write in salt adhered by tears adhered by spit adhered finally by blood. and it turned out the salt became quickly unreadable (or maybe it was eaten by evolving microorganisms, who knows?) and the blood was all that was left and the small indentations of my scraping.

and the language they derived from it was beautiful. i certainly never could have thought it up. it was not an abstract language where arbitrary markings were assigned to sounds and those sounds meant words just symbolically with no felt relation. (because how could they ever know how this sounded? how could they ever know how this felt . . . three thousand milliseconds later?)

instead they read the blood as blood. and it meant everything at once. it meant once there was water. it meant once there was birth and possible birth. it meant there were ancestors and that someone had survived. it meant life was precious and could spill. it meant spirit was sticky and could stay.

and actually that's all i was trying to say.[26]

ACKNOWLEDGMENTS

M IS FOR MULTITUDE. The waves of people known and unknown who made this possible. The living and the dead and the loud not-yet.

M IS FOR MOTHERING. This book honors the mothering of my grandmothers, Lydia Gumbs and Joyce McKenzie; my mother, Pauline McKenzie; my sister Ariana Good, who gave birth in the midst; and three of my spiritual mothers, Ifalade Tashia Asanti, Ifasade Oyade (Queen Hollins), Osunnike Ankh; and all the mothering energy named and unnamed that surrounds me.

M IS FOR MEMORY. This book is in memory of my father, Clyde Eliot Gumbs; my grandfather Joseph McKenzie; my mentors Cynthia Brown and Cheryll Greene; and my friend Tawnya Palmer.

M IS FOR MIRACLE. This book was incubating alongside my niece McKenzie Marie Good, and now she is here!

M IS FOR MAGIC. My community is Magic.

I am grateful for SpiritHouse and Warrior Healers Organizing Trust, the Durham community spaces of unconditional love and unlimited creativity that grow me and show me a black feminist reality over and over again. Thank you for embodying possibility, refusal, regeneration, and evolution all at the same time. Nia Wilson, Afiya Carter, Rachael Derello, Ebony Noelle Golden, Omisade Burney-Scott, Kriti Sharma, Mya Hunter, Matthias Pressley, Michelle Gonzales-Green, Hadassah Jones, Naeemah Kelly, Assata Goff, Sekou Goff, Heather Lee, Paul (Yusef) Newman, Adele Rose Luebke, Taj Scott, and everyone in the SpiritHouse and Warrior Healer families. Yes. Thank you.

I am grateful for all of the participants in the Brilliance Remastered online intensives and the Eternal Summer of the Black Feminist Mind Retreats and Workshops for creating a space to immerse ourselves in and be transformed by this work in process and for funding my writing life. For inspiration, insight, and support during the writing of this book, I would especially like to thank Almah LaVon Rice, Maya Freelon Asante, Eric Pritchard, Patricia Torres, Laura Sullivan, Lydia Kelow Bennett, Matice Moore, Savannah Shange, Jessica Marie Johnson, Tommi Hayes, Rockie Gilford, Ayana Omisade Flewellen, Courtney Reid-Eaton, Andrea Roberts, Bekezela Mguni, Kimalee Phillip, Lisbeth White, Lokeilan Kaimana, Samantha Taylor, Asha French, Sharifa Rhodes-Pitts, Sheena Sood, Njeri Damali Campbell, Natalie Clark, Beth Bruch, Faith Holseart, Tema Okun, Zaina Alsous, Manju Ranjendran, Emerson Zora Hamsa, Kali Ferguson, Rebeca Escalona-Rosas, Summi Dutta, Sarah Long, Shani Angela, and Xan West.

I am grateful for ALLGO and Priscilla Hale, Rose Pulliam, Omi Osun/Joni L. Jones, Sharon Bridgforth, and Karen Sanders for sponsoring and participating in an artist residency in Austin, Texas, that took this work deeper. I am grateful for the Right Relationship to Love Retreat in Anguilla, where I was able to workshop this work and come to a deeper understanding of what it was, and the Black Intimacies Salon held by Alexis De Veaux and Sokari Ekine, which was the first place I read aloud from this work. I am grateful for Janell Hobson and the "Are All the Women Still White?" panel at the National Women's Studies Association Conference in Montreal, which was the second place I read aloud from this work.

I am grateful for the facilitators and participants of the Wind and Warrior Retreat. Thank you, Ife Kilimanjaro, Karma Mayet Johnson, Nana Fofie Amina Bashir, Lisa Korantemah Pierce Williams, Abena Pierce Williams, Queen Hollins, Adela Nieves, Sarah Thompson, and everyone who danced in the rain.

I am grateful for the New Orleans Wildseeds Emergent Strategy group for growing my wildness. Infinite gratitude to Soraya Jean-Louis McElroy, Desiree Evans, and Monica McIntyre for creating the best community residency ever. I sent this manuscript into the world for the first time during that residency!

I am grateful for the Revolutionary Feminist reading group in Durham; the Black Outdoors Working Group at the John Hope Franklin Institute; Duke Gender, Sexuality and Feminist Studies in general and Priscilla Wald in particular.

I am grateful for the inspiration of so many brave black scholars and especially for the mentorship and support of Monica Miller, Farah Jasmine Griffin, Maurice Wallace, Wahneema Lubiano, Karla Holloway, Fred Moten, Sharon Holland, Mark Anthony Neal, Michelene Crichlow, Ruth Nicole Brown, Zenzele Isoke, Kim Hall, Tina Campt, Saidiya Hartman, Tavia N'yongo, Brent Edwards, Katherine McKittrick, Michelle Wright.

Mendi Obadike, M. NourbeSe Philip, Marvin K. White, and Kai Lumumba Barrow make this work imaginable.

I am grateful for all of the bookstores that welcome my work, especially Charis Books and More in Atlanta, which has claimed me as a writer since I was a teenager, and my dear friend Elizabeth Anderson, who continues the legacy of intersectional feminist transformation through stories at Charis Circle, and Chaun Webster and Verna Wong at Ancestry Books in North Minneapolis, who are creating third space with love and accountability every day. I am also very blessed by the support of local bookstores The Regulator, Flyleaf Books, and Scuppernong Books in the Durham, Triangle, and Triad area of North Carolina.

M IS FOR MAKING-IT-HAPPEN. I am so grateful for the support of everyone at Duke University Press, especially Ken Wissoker and Olivia Polk for their work with this manuscript and the generous anonymous reviewers who offered priceless insight and deep blessings. The entire team at Duke University Press including Jade Brooks, Nicole Campbell, Jessica Ryan, Heather Hensley, Chad Royal, Laura Sell, and Michael McCullough made the process of *Spill* so abundant that it expanded how I could imagine the impact of *M Archive*. Thank you to Liz Smith for your insightful and open-minded editing work on this manuscript.

And from the very beginning, M HAS BEEN FOR M. JACQUI ALEXANDER AND KITSIMBA. As Jacqui says, the message is always for the diviner. Thank you, Jacqui and Kitsimba, for creating a text that could give me something new and unexpected every day.

M IS FOR MY MAJOR MIRACLE, my champion and joy, Sangodare Akinwale/Julia Roxanne Wallace.

M IS FOR MORE. More than I can name. More of you who will come to mind as soon as I press send. More than I could have ever asked for.

NOTES

All notes in the text refer to M. Jacqui Alexander's *Pedagogies of Crossing: Meditations on Feminism, Sexual Politics, Memory, and the Sacred* (Durham, NC: Duke University Press, 2005).

PRELUDE

1 **communities (not sameness)** "Remembering," 283.

FROM THE LAB NOTEBOOKS OF THE LAST EXPERIMENTS

1 **But all things were not equal** "Anatomy of a Mobilization," 168.
2 **Being everywhere was the only way** "Pedagogies of the Sacred," 289.
3 **heart of engaged action** "Remembering," 279.
4 **Are there not fissures of class, skin color, shades of yellow and brown, within our respective nation/communities?** "Remembering," 273.
5 **No one knows the mysteries at the bottom of the ocean** "Pedagogies of the Sacred," 289.
6 **all life is shared with those at the bottom of the Ocean** "Pedagogies of the Sacred," 314.
7 **male becoming female, female becoming male** "Pedagogies of the Sacred," 289.
8 **"How would you know why the stone is there, whether you need to re- move it, bury it, or ignore it?"** "Pedagogies of the Sacred," 311.
9 **When things suffer premature death, they never concede to being put to rest** "Anatomy of a Mobilization," 151.
10 **Who are we as women of color at this moment of history?** "Remember- ing," 266.
11 **What is the threat that certain memory poses?** "Pedagogies of the Sacred," 294.
12 **Loved differently?** "Remembering," 275.

13 One of these requirements is to remember their source and purpose "Pedagogies of the Sacred," 297.

14 How do we remain committed to its different historical complexions? "Remembering," 268.

15 Do we know the terms of our different migrations? "Remembering," 274.

16 times 21 times 21 and more "Pedagogies of the Sacred," 288.

17 What is the degree of relationality between one's social location and the subject of one's theory? "Anatomy of a Mobilization," 167.

18 What kind of labor makes this intelligibility possible? "Pedagogies of the Sacred," 293.

19 to taste the opposite in things "Pedagogies of the Sacred," 289.

20 The vastness was hers alone "Anatomy of a Mobilization," 180.

21 Which truth will prevail, which dreams will be enacted? "Anatomy of a Mobilization," 179.

22 "we are here because you were there" "Remembering," 263.

23 half-written notes of paper, barely legible, now lying in overstuffed baskets, never delivered "Remembering," 274.

ARCHIVE OF DIRT: WHAT WE DID

1 even in death there are commitments and choices about the when, how and the kind of provisions with which we return "Pedagogies of the Sacred," 328.

2 avatars that make the Sacred tangible "Pedagogies of the Sacred," 299.

3 What becomes of those who cannot flee, no matter how intolerable the conditions? "Remembering," 265.

4 what will you stand for and what will you be silent about? "Anatomy of a Mobilization," 178.

5 and water to help carry the reflection of the people we wanted to become "Anatomy of a Mobilization," 178.

6 Water always remembers "Remembering," 285.

7 We have walked these dusty tracks before "Remembering," 259.

8 there is no end of paradoxes at the crossroads "Anatomy of a Mobilization," 175.

9 children into dust "Introduction," 1.

10 But we consumed without digesting "Remembering," 286.

11 let the words of my mouth and the meditation of our hearts be acceptable in thy sight "Anatomy of a Mobilization," 178.

12 **to make the taste of despair unfamiliar and therefore unwanted?** "Remembering," 269.

13 **Have we lived differently?** "Remembering," 275.

14 **and what is to be sacrificed to institute your proposal?** "Anatomy of a Mobilization," 149.

15 **With what keys are these codes activated?** "Pedagogies of the Sacred," 295.

16 **On this soil?** "Remembering," 275.

17 **Haiti?** "Remembering," 275.

18 **the realignment of self with self** "Pedagogies of the Sacred," 298.

19 **how will you be engaged in the struggle?** "Anatomy of a Mobilization," 178.

20 **but crisis is not the cause** "Pedagogies of the Sacred," 312.

21 **What archaeologies have you undertaken Jacqui?** "Remembering," 279.

22 **And how do we distinguish between those sites to which we must return and those from which we must flee entirely?** "Remembering," 265.

23 **Or do they move underground assuming a different form?** "Pedagogies of the Sacred," 294.

24 **We walk these foreign caves crouched in stealth** "Remembering," 274.

25 **each sleeping star that planned to rise to brilliance later that night** "Pedagogies of the Sacred," 321.

26 **survive above ground while really living underground by fire** "Pedagogies of the Sacred," 314.

27 **they disappeared back into the place whence they came, to await another season** "Anatomy of a Mobilization," 180.

28 **Land holds memory** "Remembering," 284.

29 **how relevant is identity and social location to the production of knowledge?** "Anatomy of a Mobilization," 166.

30 **Our hands are not clean** "Remembering," 264.

31 **How do we cultivate medicine on the forced soil of displacement** "Remembering," 269.

32 **To whom do I flee and where?** "Remembering," 268.

ARCHIVE OF SKY: WHAT WE BECAME

1 **Ultimately this alignment cannot but provoke a confrontation with history** "Pedagogies of the Sacred," 320.

2 **They walked the same celestial geography** "Pedagogies of the Sacred," 299.

3 **The dead do not like to be forgotten** "Pedagogies of the Sacred," 289.

4 reminding the body of a prior promise of its ultimate surrender "Pedagogies of the Sacred," 321.

5 **"What if we declared ourselves *perpetual* refugees in solidarity with all refugees"?** "Remembering," 265.

6 **how we came to be there and got to be who we were** "Remembering," 262.

7 **the very bodies through which divinity breathes life** "Pedagogies of the Sacred," 293.

8 **What is the self that is made in performing labor with disembodied energies that are themselves poised to work?** "Pedagogies of the Sacred," 295.

9 **a forgetting so deep, we had forgotten that we had forgotten** "Remembering," 263.

10 **Self-determination is both an individual and collective project** "Remembering," 282.

11 **once we ceased being mindless, spiritless bodies** "Anatomy of a Mobilization," 130.

12 **Trees remember and will whisper remembrances in your ear if you stay still and listen** "Remembering," 263.

13 **she can kiss you as a light breeze** "Pedagogies of the Sacred," 305.

14 **both elsewhere and here** "Introduction," 9.

15 **I had a cosmic duty to perfect my relationship with my mother** "Remembering," 260.

16 **She requires no name before her** "Remembering," 285.

ARCHIVE OF FIRE: RATE OF CHANGE

1 **we must remember the character of fire** "Remembering," 265.

2 **Have we made the crossing?** "Remembering," 275.

3 **the discipline of freedom** "Introduction," 6.

4 **candlelight as a symbol and request to see our footprints and to know the direction in which they were heading** "Anatomy of a Mobilization," 178.

5 **The idea that the fire that constitutes the center of human beings also constitutes the center of the universe anchors a Sacred connection between the two** "Pedagogies of the Sacred," 311.

6 **Our different yearnings** "Remembering," 274.

7 **What might it mean to see ourselves as "refugees of a world on fire"?** "Remembering," 264.

8 **The feel of fire is strong not hot** "Pedagogies of the Sacred," 308.

9 **an interior quality that is akin to self-possession** "Anatomy of a Mobilization," 144.

10 **Where is home?** "Remembering," 269.

11 **do what you had vowed to do in another place, another time, for another reason under different conditions** "Pedagogies of the Sacred," 314.

12 **"threading dreams, holding visions"** "Remembering," 257.

13 **disciplined freedom capable of renovating the collective terms of our engagement** "Pedagogies of the Sacred," 329.

ARCHIVE OF OCEAN: ORIGIN

1 **down in that abyss their currents reach for each other and fold, without the slightest tinge of resentment, into the same Atlantic** "Remembering," 258.

2 **only water and love** "Anatomy of a Mobilization," 162.

3 **For each thought that dared not be uttered a tear was shed** "Anatomy of a Mobilization," 178.

4 **the grieving dead instigate their global movement** "Pedagogies of the Sacred," 304.

5 **Which legacy of Pan-African lesbian feminism?** "Remembering," 275.

6 **Sentience soaks all things** "Pedagogies of the Sacred," 290.

7 **In what shape have we reached shore?** "Remembering," 275.

8 **the scent of jostled grief** "Pedagogies of the Sacred," 288.

9 **Did it coax us into the habit of listening to each other and learning each other's ways of seeing and being?** "Remembering," 275.

10 **The dead do not like to be forgotten** "Pedagogies of the Sacred," 289.

11 **our aquatic affinity with the Divine** "Pedagogies of the Sacred," 301.

12 **Where is this political movement that calls itself a women of color movement? Who mobilizes within it?** "Remembering," 266.

13 **In the distance, the echo of a pod of dolphins** "Anatomy of a Mobilization," 180.

14 **Where was my place in this new map of identity?** "Remembering," 268.

15 **We have recognized each other before** "Remembering," 273.

16 **But they did not require the Crossing in order to express beingness** "Pedagogies of the Sacred," 292.

17 **What is to be our different relationship with Africa?** "Remembering," 275.

18 **There is no crossing that is ever undertaken once and for all** "Introduction," 6.

19 **turned back at the border of self-pity** "Introduction," 17.

20 **The work of rewiring the senses is neither a single nor an individual event** "Pedagogies of the Sacred," 310.

21 **simply be within it** "Remembering," 283.

22 **Caresses all things** "Pedagogies of the Sacred," 290.

23 **a different set of waters** "Remembering," 263.

BASKETS (POSSIBLE FUTURES YET TO BE WOVEN)

1 **We petition the basket weavers to dream a new pattern of our knowing** "Remembering," 286.

2 **How do we frame our analyses, our politics, our sensibilities, our being through the chasms of those different overlapping temporalities?** "Remembering," 274.

3 **We have become familiar with the swollen face of grief that grows large in that stubborn space between love and loss** "Remembering," 274.

4 **Then and now?** "Remembering," 269.

5 **flowers from the corner grocery** "Anatomy of a Mobilization," 178.

6 **Do we remember why we made the crossing back then?** "Remembering," 275.

7 **collapsing people into buildings** "Introduction," 1.

8 **Linguistic and regional differences that have created their own insiders and outsiders?** "Remembering," 273.

9 **In whose company?** "Remembering," 275.

10 **New Orleans?** "Remembering," 275.

11 **New York?** "Remembering," 275.

12 **How do we continue to be rooted in the particularities of our cultural homes without allegiance to the boundaries of nation-states, yet remain simultaneously committed to a collectivized politic of identification and solidarity?** "Remembering," 268.

13 **cynical dress rehearsal** "Introduction," 10.

14 **There is no other work but the work of creating and re-creating ourselves within the context of community. Simply put, there is no other work** "Remembering," 283.

15 **What did it make possible? What else did we need?** "Remembering," 278.

16 **Of what is its labor constituted? What is the purpose of such labor?** "Pedagogies of the Sacred," 295.

17 **Have you lost your mind to align yourself with this Proposal?** "Anatomy of a Mobilization," 150.

18 **Are we back to square one again?** "Anatomy of a Mobilization," 174.

19 **To whom do you flee?** "Remembering," 268.

20 **What are the different intolerables from which we desire to flee?** "Remembering," 265.

21 **no signs, no visible ones at least** "Pedagogies of the Sacred," 287.

22 **division of things that belong together** "Remembering," 283.

23 **so that their vastness would seem more bearable** "Pedagogies of the Sacred," 288.

24 **How, why and under what conditions do a people remember?** "Pedagogies of the Sacred," 293–94.

25 **Who are we now, twenty years later?** "Remembering," 275.

26 **threading dreams, holding visions** "Remembering," 257 (and "Dark Sciences Dream Retreat").

27 **The Sacred is inconceivable without an aesthetic** "Pedagogies of the Sacred," 323.

28 **This dance of balance is the work of healing** "Pedagogies of the Sacred," 311.

29 **unspeakable speech is not unspeakable by some mysterious naturalizing force** "Anatomy of a Mobilization," 124.

30 **At what historical moment does heterogeneity become homogeneity— that is, the moment to create an outside enemy?** "Remembering," 273.

31 **pay the debt you were chosen to pay** "Pedagogies of the Sacred," 314.

32 **We had come this far having sung of things we most needed to learn** "Anatomy of a Mobilization," 178.

33 **they all conspired to rest their Truth everywhere** "Pedagogies of the Sacred," 289.

34 **Did *Bridge* get us there as Toni Cade Bambara believed?** "Remembering," 275.

35 **ways of seeing and being?** "Remembering," 275.

36 **Where is home? Who is family when labor means men only?** "Remembering," 269.

37 **Both change and changelessness, then, are constant** "Pedagogies of the Sacred," 292.

38 **the basement of immigrant homes** "Pedagogies of the Sacred," 291.

39 **Brazil?** "Remembering," 275.

40 **to know the body is to know it as a medium for the Divine** "Pedagogies of the Sacred," 297.

41 **Who were its cartographers?** "Remembering," 268.

1 **hydra-headed quality of violence** "Introduction," 3.

2 **Does rememory sharpen itself in the context of work, and is this project of remembering aligned with the Sacred?** "Pedagogies of the Sacred," 295.

3 **the difference between knowledge and wisdom—one could save you in the kingdom of the dead, the other gave you only temporary status in the kingdom of the living . . .** "Pedagogies of the Sacred," 315.

4 **How does one come to know oneself through and as Saints and Spirits? How does one not know oneself without them?** "Pedagogies of the Sacred," 293.

5 **What is to be the relationship with Africa in the term African American?** "Remembering," 274–75.

6 **Did she experience it, that is, witness it, or was she told about it as a common practice?** "Pedagogies of the Sacred," 309.

7 **something given as in handed, revealed** "Introduction," 7.

8 **a mobile space for the aesthetic, the poetic, the analytic, the critical, the prophetic to live all at the same time** "Anatomy of a Mobilization," 154.

9 **and who comprised that we?** "Anatomy of a Mobilization," 155.

10 **Enlivens all things** "Pedagogies of the Sacred," 290.

11 **With what in hand?** "Remembering," 275.

12 **If I am not for myself then who will be for me? But if I am *only* for myself, then what am I?** "Anatomy of a Movement," 178.

13 **my mouth open and aghast—and covered, of course** "Remembering," 260.

14 **With careful attentive service and focused contemplation the Divine is made manifest. It is why this work is never done** "Pedagogies of the Sacred," 307.

15 **for ultimately we are not our bodies and this contract cannot be settled cheaply** "Pedagogies of the Sacred," 329.

16 **hold onto what holds you up** "Pedagogies of the Sacred," 329.

17 **and water to help carry the reflection of the people we wanted to become** "Anatomy of a Mobilization," 178.

18 **reaching without need of compass for her sisters whomever and wherever they are** "Remembering," 285.

19 **energy simply does not obey the human idiom** "Pedagogies of the Sacred," 309.

20 **She will call you by your ancient name and you will answer because you will not have forgotten** "Remembering," 285.

21 **Had I not already earned the right to belong?** "Remembering," 268.

22 **How do we learn the antidote to barrenness?** "Remembering," 276.

23 **her emergence is pedagogy in its own right** "Introduction," 7.

24 **Or reincarnated in Cuba?** "Remembering," 275.

25 **the complicated undertaking of Divine self-invention** "Pedagogies of the Sacred," 300.

26 **Hieroglyphic markings to an estranged lover** "Remembering," 274.

PERIODIC KITCHEN TABLE OF ELEMENTS

The following are texts other than *Pedagogies of Crossing* with an elemental impact on this archive, organized by atomic number.

1 Ahmad, Anjail. *The Color of Memory*. Greensboro: Clear Vision Press, 1997.
2 Judd, Bettina. *Patient*. Hudson, NY: Black Lawrence Press, 2014.
3 De Veaux, Alexis. *Yabo*. Silver Spring, MD: Redbone Press, 2014.
4 Yanique, Tiphanie. *Land of Love and Drowning*. New York: Penguin, 2015.
5 Browne, Simone. *Dark Matters: On the Surveillance of Blackness*. Durham, NC: Duke University Press, 2015.
6 Shawl, Nisi. *Filter House*. Seattle: Aqueduct Press, 2008.
7 Banneker, Benjamin. Almanacs. All of them. 1792–97.
8 Madison, D. Soyini. *Acts of Activism: Human Rights as Radical Performance*. Cambridge: Cambridge University Press, 2010.
9 Osun, Omi (Joni L. Jones). *Theatrical Jazz: Performance, Ase, and the Power of the Present Moment*. Columbus: Ohio State University Press, 2015.
10 Osun, Omi (Joni L. Jones), Lisa L. Moore, and Sharon Bridgforth. *Experiments in a Jazz Aesthetic: Art, Activism, Academia, and the Austin Project*. Austin: University of Texas Press, 2010.
11 Bambara, Toni Cade. *The Salt Eaters*. New York: Knopf, 1980.
12 Ferrell, Rachelle. "Gaia." On *individuality (can i be me?)*. Capitol Records, 2000.
13 Climbing Poetree. *Ammunition*. Climbing Poetree, 2005.
14 Lorde, Audre. "The Transformation of Silence into Language and Action." In *Sister Outsider*, 40–44. Berkeley: Crossing Press, 1984.

15 Childish Gambino. "3005." On *Because the Internet*. Liberator Records, 2013.

16 Chapman, Tracy. *New Beginning*. Elektra, 1995.

17 Simpson, Leanne. *Islands of Decolonial Love*. Winnipeg: Arbeiter Ring, 2013.

18 Cymande. "Bra." On *Cymande*. Janus Records, 1972.

19 Lira. *Soul in Mind*. Giant Steps, 2009.

20 Hartman, Saidiya. *Lose Your Mother*. New York: Macmillan, 2007.

21 Sweet Honey in the Rock. *Sweet Honey in the Rock Tribute LIVE at Lincoln Center*. Appleseed Records, 2013.

22 Spillers, Hortense. *Black, White, and in Color: Essays on American Culture*. Chicago: University of Chicago Press, 2003.

23 Anzaldua, Gloria. *Borderlands/La Frontera: The New Mestiza*. San Francisco: Aunt Lute Press, 1987.

24 Simone, Nina. "22nd Century." On *Sugar in My Bowl: The Very Best of Nina Simone 1969–1972*. Sony Legacy, 1998.

25 Madison, D. Soyini, ed. *The Woman That I Am*. New York: St. Martin's Press, 1997.

26 Humez, Jean. *Harriet Tubman: The Life and Life Stories*. Madison: University of Wisconsin Press, 2006.

27 KING. *We Are KING*. KING CREATIVE, 2016.

28 Simone, Nina. "Sinnerman." On *Pastel Blues*. Philips Records, 1965.

29 Boggs, Grace Lee. *The Next American Revolution: Sustainable Activism for the 21st Century*. Berkeley: University of California Press, 2012.

30 Yancey, James (J Dilla/Jay Dee). *Fuck the Police*. Up Above Records, 2001.

31 Hamer, Fannie Lou. *Songs My Mother Taught Me*. Smithsonian Folkway Records, 2015.

32 BoyzIIMen. "Can You Stand the Rain" (acapella cover). On *Evolution*. Motown, 1997.

33 Hartmann, Ivor. "Last Wave." In *Jalada*, January 15, 2015. Accessed December 28, 2016. https://jalada.org/2015/01/15/last-wave-by-ivor-w-hartmann/.

34 June, Valerie. "Astral Plane." On *The Order of Time*. Concord Bicycle Records, 2017.

35 Butler, Octavia. *Parable of the Sower*. New York: Warner, 1993.

36 Okorafor, Nnedi. *Who Fears Death*. New York: Penguin, 2011.

37 Harding, Rosemarie Freeney, and Rachel Elizabeth Harding.

Remnants: A Memoir of Spirit, Activism, and Mothering. Durham, NC: Duke University Press, 2015.

38 Painter, Nell. *Sojourner Truth: A Life, a Symbol.* New York: Norton, 1996.

39 Uzuri, Imani. *Her Holy Water: A Black Girl's Rock Opera.* New York: Her Holy Water Music, 2007.

40 Woods, Jamila. HEAVN. Jamila Woods, 2016.

41 Ndegeocello, Meshell. "Aquarium." On *The Spirit Music Jamia: Dance of the Infidel.* Shanachie Records, 2005.

42 McIntyre, Monica. *It Soon Come.* Monica McIntyre Music, 2013.

43 Wonder, Stevie. *Songs in the Key of Life.* Motown, 1976.

44 R.E.M. "E-bow the Letter." On *New Adventures in Hi-Fi.* Warner Brothers, 1996.

45 Rihanna. "Same Old Mistakes." On *Anti.* Westbury Road, 2016.

46 Verdelle, A. J. *The Good Negress.* Chapel Hill, NC: Algonquin Books, 1995.

47 Cortez, Jayne. *Within These Circles: Literature of African Women Writers.* Carbondale: Southern Illinois University Press, 1994.

48 Whitehead, Colson. *The Intuitionist.* New York, Knopf, 2012.

49 Osunlade. *Beats de los Muertos.* Yoruba Records, 2010.

50 Anzaldua, Gloria, and Cherríe Moraga, eds. *This Bridge Called My Back: Writings by Radical Women of Color.* Boston: Kitchen Table: Women of Color Press, 1981.

51 Blackalicious. *Blazing Arrow.* MCA, 2002.

52 Naylor, Gloria. *Bailey's Café.* New York: Vintage Books, 1992.

53 Jean, Wyclef. "Apocalypse." On *The Carnival.* Ruffhouse, 1997.

54 Greene, Cheryll, and William Strickland. *Malcolm X: Make It Plain.* New York: Penguin, 1995.

55 Shange, Ntozake. *Sassafrass, Cypress and Indigo.* New York: St. Martin's Press, 1982.

56 Bambara, Toni Cade, ed. *The Black Woman.* New York: New American Library, 1970.

57 Mvula, Laura. *Live with the Metropole Orkest at Abbey Road Studio.* London: Sony, 2014.

58 Bell's Roar. *Bell's Roar.* Mondo Tunes, 2014.

59 Lara, Ana-Maurine. *Erzulie's Skirt.* Silver Spring, MD: Redbone Press, 2004.

60 Ndegeocello, Meshell. *Comet Come to Me.* Naïve, 2014.

61 Coltrane, Alice. *Ptah the El Daoud*. Impulse Records, 1970.
62 Weisman, Alan. *The World without Us*. New York: Macmillan, 2007.
63 Murray, Pauli. *Dark Testament and other Poems*. New York: Silvermine, 1970.
64 Mire, Hawa Y. "Black Woman, Everybody's Healer." In *Jalada*, January 15, 2015. Accessed December 31, 2016. https://jalada.org/2015/01/15/black-woman-everybodys-healer-by-hawa-y-mire/.
65 Nelson, Alondra. *The Social Life of DNA*. Boston: Beacon Press, 2016.
66 Moten, Fred, and Stefano Harney. *Undercommons: Fugitive Planning and Black Study*. Brooklyn: Autonomedia, 2013.
67 Smith, Barbara, ed. *Home Girls: A Black Feminist Anthology*. Boston: Kitchen Table: Women of Color Press, 1983.
68 Richardson, Cheddie. Driftwood Haven Studio. Anguilla. Accessed December 31, 2016. http://news.ai/web/cheddie/.
69 Jeffers, Honorée. *The Age of Phillis*. Forthcoming.
70 Georgakas, Dan, and Marvin Surkin. *Detroit, I Do Mind Dying*. New York: St. Martin's Press, 1975.
71 Brown, Cynthia. *From Cynthia with Love: Reflections on Living with Cancer*. Forthcoming.
72 Lorde, Audre. *The Cancer Journals*. San Francisco: Spinsters/Aunt Lute, 1980.
73 Condé, Maryse. *I, Tituba, Black Witch of Salem*. New York: Ballantine, 1994.
74 Lorde, Audre. *Our Dead behind Us*. New York: Norton, 1986.
75 Shockley, Evie. *a half-red sea*. Chapel Hill, NC: Carolina Wren Press, 2006.
76 Moraga, Cherríe, Alma Gómez, and Mariana Roma-Carmera, eds. *Cuentos: Stories by Latinas*. Latham, NY: Kitchen Table: Women of Color Press, 1983.
77 Bell, Derrick. "The Space Traders." In Sheree R. Thomas, ed. *Dark Matter: A Century of Speculative Fiction from the African Diaspora*, 326–55. New York: Warner, 2000. Orig. pub. 1992.
78 Philip, M. NourbeSe, *Looking for Livingstone: An Odyssey of Silence*. London: Mercury Press, 1991.
79 Arewa, Caroline Shola. *Opening to Spirit: Contacting the Healing Power of the Chakras and Honouring African Spirituality*. London: Horsons, 1998.
80 Boggs, James, and Grace Lee. *Revolution and Evolution in the 20th Century*. New York: New York University Press, 1974.

81 Lorde, Audre. *Zami: A New Spelling of My Name*. Berkeley: Crossing Press, 1982.

82 Gomez, Jewelle. *The Gilda Stories*. Ithaca: Firebrand Books, 1991.

83 Bambara, Toni Cade. "Madame Bai and the Taking of Stone Mountain." In *Deep Sightings and Rescue Missions*, 27–44. New York: Random House, 1996.

84 Jackson, Mahalia. "How I Got Over (Live)." On *The Best of Mahalia Jackson*. Sony/Legacy, 1995.

85 Parks, Sheri. *Fierce Angels: The Strong Black Woman in American Life and Culture*. New York: Ballantine, 2010.

86 Ra, Sun. *Space Is the Place*. Dir. John Coney. 1974.

87 Terell, JoAnn Marie. *Power in the Blood? The Cross in the African American Experience*. Eugene, OR: Wipf and Stock, 2005.

88 Hull, Akasha Gloria. *Soul Talk: The New Spirituality of African American Women*. Rochester, VT: Inner Traditions, 2001.

89 Edwards, Erica. *Charisma and the Fictions of Black Leadership*. Minneapolis: University of Minnesota Press, 2012.

90 Chancy, Myriam. *The Loneliness of Angels*. Kingston: Peepal Tree Press, 2010.

91 Generation 5. *Toward Transformative Justice: A Liberatory Approach to Child Sexual Abuse and Other Forms of Intimate and Community Violence*. San Francisco: Generation 5, 2007.

92 Brown, Adrienne Maree. *Emergent Strategy: Shaping Change, Changing Worlds*. Oakland: AK Press, 2017.

93 Greenberg, Gary. *A Grain of Sand*. Minneapolis: Voyageur Press, 2008.

94 Beinfield, Harriet, and Efrem Korngold. *Between Heaven and Earth: A Guide to Chinese Medicine*. New York: Ballantine, 1991.

95 Guy-Sheftall, Beverly, Stanlie M. James, and Frances Smith Foster. *Still Brave: The Evolution of Black Women's Studies*. New York: Feminist Press, 2009.

96 Silko, Leslie Marmon. *Almanac of the Dead*. New York: Penguin, 1991.

97 Onofrio, Alba. "The Day After." Sermon at Vanderbilt University. Accessed December 29, 2016. https://www.youtube.com/watch?v=lK2cQbVGHBA.

98 Butler, Octavia. *Parable of the Talents*. New York: Warner, 1998.

99 Prince. *1999*. Warner Brothers, 1982.

100 Jackson, Mahalia. *Down by the Riverside*. Recorded in 1968 in Antibes, France. Released by Golden Options in multiple editions.

101 Res. *How I Do.* MCA, 2001.
102 Marshall, Paule. *Praisesong for the Widow.* New York: Penguin, 1983.
103 Brodber, Erna. *Jane and Louisa Will Soon Come Home.* London: New Beacon Press, 1980.
104 Flaherty, Jordan. *Floodlines: Community and Resistance from Katrina to the Jena Six.* Chicago: Haymarket Press, 2010.
105 Marley, Robert Nester. "Redemption Song." On *Uprising.* Island Records, 1980.
106 Green, Jaki Shelton. "I Know the Grandmother One Had Hands." In *Conjure Blues.* Chapel Hill, NC: Carolina Wren Press, 1996.
107 Brodber, Erna. *Myal.* London: New Beacon Press, 1988.
108 Okparanta, Chinelo. *Happiness, Like Water.* New York: Houghton Mifflin Harcourt, 2013.
109 Brodber, Erna. *Louisiana.* Jackson: University Press of Mississippi, 1994.
110 Tchaikovsky, Adrian. "Children of Dagon." *Lightspeed Magazine*, no. 65 (October 2015). Accessed December 28, 2016. http://www.light speedmagazine.com/fiction/children-of-dagon/.
111 Kincaid, Jamaica. *At the Bottom of the River.* New York: Macmillan, 1983.
112 Hopkinson, Nalo. *The Salt Roads.* New York: Warner, 2003.
113 Hughes, Langston. *The Big Sea.* New York: Knopf, 1940.
114 Borges, Jorge Luis. *Labyrinths.* New York: New Directions, 1961.
115 L'Engle, Madeleine. *The Arm of the Starfish.* New York: Macmillan, 1965.
116 Complex Movements. *Beware of the Dandelions.* Detroit: Emergence Media, 2014. Accessed December 28, 2016. https://emergencemedia .org/pages/beware-of-the-dandelions.
117 Sharma, Kriti. *Interdependence.* New York: Fordham University Press, 2015.
118 Imarisha, Walidah, and Adrienne Maree Brown, eds. *Octavia's Brood: Science Fiction Stories from Social Justice Movements.* Oakland: AK Press, 2015.